A.J.M. SMITH

Romantic Exuberance

A.J.M. SMITH

Romantic Exuberance

V. Lakshmanan

AUTHORSPRESS
Publishers of Scholarly Books

Worldwide Circulation through Authorspress Global Network

First Published 2011
by
Authorspress

Editorial
Q-2A Hauz Khas Enclave,
New Delhi-110 016
e-mail: authorspress@yahoo.com

Marketing
E-35/103, Jawahar Park
Laxmi Nagar, Delhi-110 092
e-mail: authorspress@yahoo.com

A.J.M. Smith: Romantic Exuberance
ISBN 978-81-7273-537-1

Printed in India at Tarun Offset, Delhi.

Preface

A.J.M. Smith led a movement for literary nationalism in Canada. He endeavoured to bring about a change in Canadian poetry from late-Victorian form of verse to classical modernism. In this process, his instinctive romanticism was in conflict with his professed modernism. A continuous attempt to balance a conflicting sensibility divided over the contradictory desire to hold an exuberant romantic loveliness and to sluice of it in lonely austerity is a recurrent pattern in his poetry. In the romantic-modernist dialectics, he remains modernist on principle while his poems actually swerve towards romanticism. His modernism is, then, a reaction against his romantic self. This conflict is the essence of his poetry.

Smith's poetry eventually is a verbal dutchman. (A dutchman, in carpentry, is a wedge inserted to hide the fault in a badly made joint; in theatre, it is a narrow strip of canvas to conceal the joint between two flats; in a more general sense, it connotes something fleetingly and fragilely held together that provides the illusion of solidity and permanence.) In his satires and pastorals, and other such less 'felt' poems the façade of strict modernity donned by Smith is perfect and harmonious. It is in his intensely 'felt' and strongly 'emoted' poems that this faultless façade is relentlessly stripped away. My object in this book is to discover the romantic niches in his modernist poetry, and to evaluate his exuberant romantic sensibility.

Smith is concerned with the permanence of art, and takes meticulous care that his poems are made to last. His published poetry is slim in volume because he was an exigent critic of his own poems. Based on a study of publication details of 195 poems of Smith in the annotated bibliography of him by Anne Burke, it is found that his first poem "Sonnet" was published in 1921, his fiftieth poem in 1925, his one-hundredth poem in 1928, his hundred-and-fiftieth poem in 1957 and his last poem in 1978. It is obvious that half of his total output was achieved in less than eight years between 1921 and 1928, and the remaining half in fifty years between 1928 and 1978. He has had a very boisterous, creative period during 1921-28, but, after that, his attempts at poetry had been patchy. Instead, he had indulged in revision of his poems. About twenty per cent of his canon—comprising mainly the poems for which he is best-known—has undergone major changes at some time in his career. The trend in his revisions is always toward the removal of romantic diction and the substitution of impersonal images and imaginative language. On all such occasions, paradoxically, his romantic sensibility becomes glaring, much more perceptible.

Smith exhibits a wide range of styles and themes in his poems. His versatility has often proved an obstruction to critics seeking unity of tone and purpose in his poetry. The earliest of his poems to gain recognition were heavily indebted to Yeats and Eliot. "The Lonely Land" and "Like an Old Proud King in a Parable" are the most anthologized poems of this period. "The Lonely Land" is widely admired for its precise evocation of the Canadian North. "Proud Parable" is expressive of the conflicting romantic-modernist sensibility in the poet. During the middle period of his career, in the 1930s, he turned to poetry that dealt with social and political issues. "News of the Phoenix" is the best example of his satirical poems; its double edged irony is remarkable. In two other poems of this period, "Far West" and "Noctambule," he is very complex, demanding the reader's ability to identify and appreciate a wide range of allusions that underlie an apparently surreal vision. These works give credence to his metaphysical qualities, not only in their juxtaposition of seemingly unrelated images but also in their fusion of intellect and feeling, abstract ideas and human emotions. In his later poetry, he dwells increasingly on the theme of death. Two poems of this period, "Metamorphosis" and "The Wisdom of Old Jelly Roll," with images of sensuality and regeneration, highlight his unshakeable commitment to life. The same theme is most lovingly and dynamically explored in "The Archer," considered his finest poem by many. His poetry is evidently a metaphorical journey from dissonance to assonance, a lyrical flight from agony to ecstasy, a symbolic expedition from non-life to life.

I have attempted to locate the poetry of this gifted and enigmatic poet within the context of national and international poetry in this book. I have adopted the teleological structure of tracing the evolution of Smith from romanticism to modernism and to mimesis, and then a fusion of various strands at the end. I thought it a useful template because while the various stages of his poetic career have been noticed by other critics, no one has dealt with the complexities of each phase with much clarity and depth. I have discussed him in the larger traditions of British and American poetry, and attempted to reinforce dominant patterns, and also point to the various antinomies in each phase of his poetic career. My instinctive facility for close textual reading has enabled me to see the inconsistencies and struggles of a poet trying to express his private vision within a larger cultural context.

The introductory chapter, *In Search of a Distinct Canadian Identity: Smith's Eclectic Modernism,* briefly traces the progress made by Canadian poets in their quest for a nationalistic literary tradition. It also narrates the evolution of Smith's poetics, its distinguishing features and his literary accomplishments. The second chapter, *A Meadow in the Northern Stone,* makes a study of Smith's earliest poems and the lapidary poems he turned out later. It is observed that there is a good deal of romanticism with strong reverberations of Keats in his poetry of this period. The third chapter, *Sharpness Cutting Sharpness,* emphasizes the imagist precision in his poetry. His imagistic concepts undergo shades of change from conventional imagism of Henri Bergson and T.E. Hulme. These imagists captured the objects and communicated the things perceived through images. But Smith adds an analytical clause to this conventional process, and presents objects in relation and in flux. The fourth chapter, *A Bandolier Full of Kodak Films,* attempts to evaluate the satiric intent in his poems of invective. He satirizes the manners of Canadians but he does not carry on a jeremiad like his eighteenth century English exemplars. The fifth chapter, *In a Sort of Ecstasy,* describes the humorous break in his serious poetic career when he is seen to celebrate the hilarious, "festive moments" of life. His love-lyrics and light-verses written during this phase of his life are characteristic of life—exuberance, humanity and colloquial diction appropriate for such an occasion. In his festive poetry, he engages himself with the idea of the pastoral. His engagement with the pastoral form is related with vital questions of how the Canadian landscape like the American is constantly being threatened by technology, by the machine in the garden; questions about what exactly is Smith's attitude to technical progress and what is his feeling about nature are raised. The sixth chapter, *To Be Nothing is To Be All,* deals with his poems on death and his metaphysical concerns where there is an onward progression from death-fear to death-recognition. The seventh concluding chapter defends him from the criticism of "inconsistency."

As a critic of his own poetry, Smith had always discouraged the identification of poet and persona. True to his feelings, his critics have been writing "The speaker says" or "The persona of the poem says"; never have they written "Smith says" or "The poet says." However, in this book, I have at all times used "Smith says" or "The poet says" for reasons of ease and readability. I have also made other similar adjustments and adaptations simplifying things for the common reader.

The book is written, designed and laid out to draw three categories of readers. Firstly, it is prepared as a sourcebook for prospective scholars who intend to do serious research on Smith or Canadian modernism. It is designed as a comprehensive handbook on a single characteristic of Smith: his poetry is presented as a mishmash of the romantic and the modern where the romantic exuberance ultimately stands out. Secondly, many of the Indian universities have now introduced Canadian literature in their curriculum and very often Smith's poetry forms an important component of the syllabus. This book is laid out especially as a general guidebook to such first generation learners/popular readers of Canadian poetry.

Thirdly, it might also serve as a reference manual to Smith's poems as 44 of his commonly anthologized poems have been closely analysed under their titles. An index of these titles is appended to the book. It is hoped that this book will be of interest to readers and scholars of poetry.

I thank my wife, Dr. V. Radha, Professor of Economics, Annamalai University, my daughter Dr. Sugirdha Prakash, a dentist in Singapore, and my son, Nikkhil Charan, Creative Head of Big Perks, a publishing-house in Singapore, for their suggestions, particularly in improving the readability of the book. They have been my first readers and best critics.

I thank ECW Press for allowing me to use the cover image from their copyrighted materials.

I express my appreciation and thankfulness to my friend and publisher, Sudarshan Kcherry, Authorspress, for making this book ubiquitous.

Above all, with all humility, I thank God for all His kindness.

V.Lakshmanan

Contents

1

In Search of a Distinct Canadian Identity: Smith's Eclectic Modernism

In the years that ushered in the twentieth century the direction that the poetry of this century would take – poetic modernism—was established. "On or about 1910, human nature changed," said Virginia Woolf. It is true that in the years thereabout much changed in human nature and the social order and in the techniques of literary art. Modernism, in literature, relates to the contemporary writers' visions of human society and the revolutionary devices they invented to represent these visions in literature. Poetic modernism, then, relates to the attempts made by the poets to express the discontinuous nature of contemporary life. The conventional features of a well-made poem – consistency of style, rationality of structure, and steadiness of viewpoint – cannot represent the illogicality of our modern-day lives. Hence in the modernistic and experimental tradition that followed, there is a deliberate attempt to go beyond conventional notions of continuity and design, to make the poem a record of modern life's discontinuities. Postmodernism and the very recent sound poetry and concrete poetry are all off-shoots of modernism; it can reversely be established that modernism is only "proto-postmodernism" (Shyamal Bagchee, 191).

Modernism, like romanticism, came late to Canada in the 1920s. The first rather make-shift experiments in Canada in poetic modernism began in 1914 when Arthur Stringer presented his free-verse collection *Open Water*. E. J. Pratt, who stood in time between the Confederation poets and the moderns, showed his kinship with the moderns by his complexity and consistent reflectivity. But a truly consistent expression of modernist principles occurred only during 1924 when a configuration of circumstance and career brought F.R. Scott, Smith and Leon Edel to McGill University, who were later joined by A.M. Klein and Leo Kennedy to form the "Montreal group." Together they were responsible for founding and editing *The McGill Fortnightly Review* in 1925 which represented the innovative spirit of the 1920s in Canada. Leon Edel recalls Smith's influence on him at the time:

> We would sit at the back of a class-room and pretend to listen . . . while Smith wrote poems and gave me T. S. Eliot to read. . . . Smith first taught me the meaning of literature. . . . He made me feel the modern idiom, the use of this year's language shorn of the old accretions of meaning. (Quoted in Francis, 301)

Smith's central impulse, evidently, was that of a teacher, "a poet's poet," in the propagation of modernism in Canada, like that of Pound elsewhere. Hyatt H. Waggoner writes of Pound:

> Pound taught and promoted many others besides Williams and Eliot. . . . In the early years especially, he cultivated friends and used them without apology to get done what he thought must be done, at first to save poetry from romanticism and idealism, later to make his influence felt toward saving a botched civilization. (391)

Smith was widely read in the new poetry of Eliot, Yeats and Pound and was distressed to notice a lack of technical and intellectual seriousness among contemporary Canadian poets. His preference for the "poetry of ideas" to the "poetry of feeling" is evident in the concluding lines of his explosive article "Wanted: Canadian Criticism" (1928):

> Modernity and tradition alike demand that the contemporary artist who survives adolescence shall be an intellectual. Sensibility is no longer enough, intelligence is also required. Even in Canada. (169)

Smith's modernism – a curious combination of Eliot's classicism and Yeatsian romanticism – is indeed eclectic and makes an ambitious bid to exist within the artifice of eternity. His preference for the "cosmopolitan" to the "native" has often been criticized, but the native against which he rebelled was not the achievement represented by the best of the Confederation poets but "the maple-and-beaver references of a self-conscious pseudo-nationalism" (Keith 62).

Smith's modernism made a profound impact on modern Canadian poetry. He is undoubtedly one of the founders of the modern literary movement in Canada. Critics of his own vintage have attributed admirable epithets to him like "doyen of Canadian letters," "aesthetic master of Canadian poetry" and "Canadian Yeats." But the other side also existed. Critics sometimes identified him with the austere protagonists of his poems and called him "lapidary" and "ascetic." To them, Smith was fond of quoting a line from Rimbaud: *"Je est un autre."* He writes further: "My poems are not autobiographical, subjective or personal. None of them is reverie, confession or direct self-expression. They are fiction, drama, art; sometimes pastiche, sometimes burlesque and sometimes respectful parody" ("A Self-Review": *Towards a View,* 215).

A distinct English literary tradition in Canada dates back to the middle of the eighteenth century. The English explorers and pioneer writers found the English language and its poetry inadequate to express their very different Canadian experience. J. MacKay writes in *Quebec Hill* (1797):

> Ye who, in stanzas, celebrate the Po,
> Or teach the Tyber in your strains to flow,
> How would you toil for numbers to proclaim
> The liquid grandeur of St. Lawrence stream?

Aspiring poets like MacKay were concerned about the impact of the British and American traditions upon Canadian poetry and were in continual quest for a distinct Canadian tradition.

In 1867, a few states in North America joined together and confederated into a nation called Canada. This year is called the Year of Confederation. The four poets, C. D. Roberts, Bliss Carman, Archibald Lampman and D. C. Scott, who lived and wrote during these years, are called the Confederation poets. For all practical purposes, Canadian poetry can be said to begin with these four poets. These poets initially wrote a conservative and romantic mode of verse; they turned to such poets as Byron, Wordsworth, Shelley and Keats for their models. But their later poetry laid firm foundation for a tradition of Canadian poetry. This gradually developed into a distinct native style of poetry.

E.J. Pratt stood in time between the Confederation poets and the Canadian modernists. He provided an essential link between the attitudes and assumptions of the Confederation poets on the one hand and modernist principles and practice on the other. It took Canadians a long time to come to terms with modernism, the poetic revolution of the early twentieth century associated with the names of Ezra Pound and T.S. Eliot. Pratt's poetry can be seen as bridging the gap between the traditional and the contemporary. Pratt demonstrated his kinship with the Confederation poets by his show of masculine force in rhyme, by his love of narrative and by the nature of his moral concerns. He established his association with the moderns by his complexity and consistent reflectivity and by the steps he took towards a considered solution of the modern problem. Pratt moved with comparative ease between the two worlds.

During the early 1920s, A.J.M. Smith, F.R. Scott, A.M. Klein and Leo Kennedy gathered together at McGill University to form the "Montreal Group" or the "McGill Movement." Commenting on the formation of the McGill Movement under the leadership of Smith, Smith's biographer Wynne Francis writes: "Smith's enthusiasm, combined with his critical, creative and carry-forward talents made him the leader of the first concerted effort to establish the new Poetry in Canada" (301).

The members of the "Montreal Group" came together, however, only to propagate modernism. In other aspects their work showed heterogeneity. F.R. Scott was influenced by

W.H. Auden and Stephen Spender for his satiric spirit; W.W.E. Ross and Ezra Pound for his imagism; and Whitman for his popular poetry. A.M. Klein configured his poetry from Jewish Chassidism, English Jacobean writers and James Joyce. Leo Kennedy showed a curious combination of the influence of John Webster and Emily Dickinson. Smith learned from Yeats, T.S. Eliot and Pound; from the Metaphysical poets Herbert and Vaughan; and from early French modernists like Laforgue and Mallarme.

Three literary movements – romanticism, modernism and postmodernism – merge in Smith's poetry. In the romantic-modernist dialectics, Smith remains modernist on principle, while his poems actually throw the balance of feeling a little towards romanticism. His modernism is in part a reaction against his romantic self. This conflict is the essence of his poetry.

When we look at Smith's broad poetic qualities, we find that three things dominate his poetry: life-affirming optimism, conflicting sensibility and landscape patriotism. Generally, Canadian writers prefer to be pessimistic. Margaret Atwood writes in *Survival*:

> Canadian authors spend a disproportionate amount of time making sure that their heroes die or fail. Much Canadian writing suggests that failure is required because it is felt – consciously or unconsciously – to be the only 'right' ending, the only thing that will support the character's or author's view of the universe. . . . Given a choice of the negative or positive aspects of any symbol – sea as life-giving Mother, sea as what your ship goes down in; tree as symbol of growth, tree as what falls on your head – Canadians show a marked preference for the negative. (34-5)

But Smith was an exception. He was overtly positive. His poetry is analogous balancing of joy in life-force and happiness in depressive visions; it is music of opposing tones, joyous and melancholic, and at the same time remarkably impersonal. Smith's life-affirming qualities include a love of nature and love of native landscape, a longing for perfection in art, a fascination for existential pleasures and ecstatic moments of life and a nostalgic dreaminess of the past.

Smith is concerned with the permanence of art, and takes meticulous care that his work is made to last. He championed the exercise of critical intelligence, the fusion of thought and feeling, respect for poetic craftsmanship, above all, precise diction:

> To hold in a verse as austere
> As the spirit of prairie and river,
> Lonely unburyable, dear
> The North, as a deed, and forever.
>
> ("To Hold in a Poem")

Smith's obsession with the mythical North in this poem, and in other poems, has greater association with the central pattern of Canadian poetry which is the evocation of a sense of stark terror. The immediate cause of this sense of terror is the North Canadian landscape. When the early European settlers came to Canada either via Hudson Bay or the Gulf of St. Lawrence they landed in a lush green, verdant land. But as they travelled north, the huge, magnified Canadian landscape wrapped and swallowed them up. These Canadian settlers, once engulfed and surrounded, got frightened and confounded of nature around them. Their first reaction to the northern landscape therefore was that of terror, the frightening loneliness of a huge and thinly populated country. To set things right, Smith, prompted by intense nationalism and landscape patriotism, encourages the Canadians to migrate to the north. He tells that even though the northern part of Canada is stony, it is stunningly and strikingly beautiful. There is rarely a poem of Smith where the mythical northern stone does not appear.

The mythical Canadian north is also associated with the evolution of modernism in Canada. The beginnings of modernism in Canada coincided with a revival of cultural nationalism. This national spirit accelerated a desire in the native people for a truly distinctive Canadian art and literature which would confirm the existence of a Canadian nationality. The answer to such a desire was to be found in the fusion of a distinctly Canadian landscape and alien modernist techniques. This brought to focus a myth identifying Canada with her northern geography.

In the words of the national anthem, Canada was "the true north, strong and free." In the words of Haliburton, Canadians were "the North men of the New World." In Scott's poem entitled "The Height of Land," Canada was "The Lonely north . . . / Glimmering all night / In the arctic light." Added to these were the new visions of the canvas and collage generated by the Group of Seven painters which showed the Canadian landscape as vast, strong, lonely, and above all, northern. In 1936, August Bridle, in a review discussing both an exhibition of the Group of Seven paintings and the publication of *New Provinces,* the first anthology of Canadian modernist poetry, goes so far as to argue that the painters rather than the poets were the first Canadian modernists. "So the painters," he writes, "were the pace-makers of modernism in Canada" (quoted in Djwa, "A New Soil and a Sharp Sun", 15).

Smith's published poetry is slim in volume because he was an exigent critic of his own poems. He has had a very boisterous creative period during 1921-30, but, after that, his attempts at poetry are patchy. Based on a study of publication details of 195 poems of Smith in the annotated bibliography of Smith by Anne Burke, it is found that his first poem "Sonnet" was published in 1921, his fiftieth poem in 1925, his one-hundredth poem in 1928, his hundred-and-fiftieth poem in 1957 and his last poem in 1978. It can be seen that half of his total output was achieved in less than eight years between 1921 and 1928 and the remaining half in fifty years between 1928 and 1978. E.J. Pratt predicted this slow-down as early as 1944 in "Canadian Poets in the U.S.A":

> . . . hope that he [Smith's] will not slow down his output in poetry, for it is in this creative field that his sensitive craftsmanship will yield the best grain. (35)

Instead, Smith indulged in revision of his poems. About twenty per cent of his canon –comprising mainly the poems for which he is best-known – has undergone major changes at some time in his career. Borrowing from his own works is a common aspect of Smith's revisions. He took the phrase "staggers and falls" from "Something Apart" and used it, slightly altered, in a revised version of "The Lonely Land." Among other changes, in "Ode: On the Death of William Butler Yeats" he altered the commonplace "The bird has sought the mountain top" to the more complex "The white swan plummets the mountain top," which is rare for its unusual and imaginative usage of the word "plummet" as a verb. "Far West" shows a progressive alteration in the penultimate line, from "girl-smooth horses" to "girl-sleek horses" to the more satisfyingly alliterative "skin-tight stallions."

The main purpose of these revisions is Smith's love for excellence. His devotion for perfection is clearly stated in one of his poems where he counsels a younger writer to aim at achieving the effect "of a hard thing done / Perfectly, as though without care." He observes in the essay "The Poetic Process": "I suppose I am what is called an academic poet. The finished work rather than the work of finishing is what I have valued most" (*Towards a View,* 224). To the people who still regard poetry as a high art, "pure, timeless and absolute," Smith's exquisitely crafted poems are among the best of their kind in any literature.

Smith was born on 8 November 1902 of British parents, Octavius Arthur Smith and Alexandra Louise Whiting, in Westmount, Quebec. He attended Westmount High School. He discovered modern poetry when, as a teenager, he came across Harriet Monroe and Alice Corbin Henderson's *New Poetry: An Anthology* (1917) in the Westmount Public Library. He shares with Michael Heenan of this experience:

> In 1920 at Westmont High I began to read modern poetry . . . before that I read Tennyson, and Shelley and Keats. At school I used to read under my desk *Poems of the Romantic Revival* – Shelley and Keats and Byron – when we should have been doing geography or learning how much coffee was produced in Brazil and that sort of thing. (Heenan: online)

When Smith went to England to stay with his parents during 1918-20 he frequented bookshops in London and read much of "Pound, Eliot, Yeats, Sitwell and Stevens." He was already imitating these writers when he returned to Canada and entered McGill University in 1921. He registered as a science student, but a course in seventeenth century English literature strengthened his love for poetry. He was strongly drawn to the metaphysical poets and found Marvell and Vaughan congenial to his own outlook.

With the awareness of the concerns of modernism in other parts of the world the young Smith turned his attention to Canadian poetry. The reigning poets, G.D. Roberts, Lampman and Pratt did not inspire him. These poets favoured a more conventional approach to poetry. Smith despised this "Maple Leaf School" of poets. During 1924, as editor of the Literary Supplement of McGill *Daily*, Smith began his campaign to establish modernism in Canada. He tells Heenan of this venture:

> We were just having a lot of fun getting some of the kind of poetry that we liked written and published as a kind of reaction against the conventional, romantic, maple-leaf, Bliss Carman sort of poetry. We were rather strong for imagism because of its conciseness. (Heenan: online)

By this time, F.R. Scott was also at McGill. Scott and Smith formed an immediate friendship. Together they were responsible for founding and editing *The McGill Fortnightly Review* in 1925, which represented the innovative spirit of the 1920s in Canada. Among the two, Scott has, on more than one occasion, referred to Smith's enduring influence on him. Recalling the McGill days, Scott writes in "Arthur James Marshall Smith: A Memoir": "I was on the road to Damascus but his [Smith's] was the light that suddenly shone upon me. He showed the wonders of a world I had been missing" (quoted in Burke, 329). In an interview with Kathleen Moore, Scott gratefully remembers Smith introducing him to the work of Eliot, Pound, Cummings and Williams (Kathleen Moore, 5-10). Established critical evaluations have recognized Scott only as a superb social satirist, whereas Smith is acknowledged as the pioneer of a tradition. Later, *The McGill Fortnightly Review* drew to it other young writers like A.M. Klein and Leo Kennedy on whom Smith exerted an enduring influence.

Smith graduated from McGill in 1925. He completed his post-graduate degree in the same university in 1926 with a dissertation on *The Poetry of W.B. Yeats.* He married Jeannie Dougall Robins. He got a teacher-fellowship for study in the University of Edinburgh in 1927. He spent two years at Edinburgh where he studied under H.J.C. Grierson, who brought out a famous edition of the metaphysical poets. While in Edinburgh, Smith continued to write and publish poems in the leading American, British and Canadian journals. Some of his popular poems, "Prothalamium," "The Creek" and "Like an Old Proud King in a Parable" were published during these years. The first serious commentary of Smith's poems was made by Raymond Knister in 1927 who referred to Smith's poems as "some of the most promising now in evidence in his generation" (6).

Smith's contentious article, "Wanted-Canadian Criticism," appeared in *The Canadian Forum* in 1928. Like T.S. Eliot's "Tradition and the Individual Talent" which changed the course of creativity and criticism of poetry in England and America, Smith's "Wanted-Canadian Criticism" changed the course of poetry-writing and criticism in Canada. It stressed upon the indispensability of a special and peculiar brand of Canadian poetry and Canadian literature which must be judged by established standards. The article was a ruthless condemnation of the absence of innovation in contemporary Canadian poetry and an urgent call for higher and more stringent creativity based on "internationally recognized aesthetic criteria." The article insisted upon the fact that an existing literature was guided by its existing tradition, whereas a new literature was without a tradition of its own, "One looks in vain through Canadian books and journals for that critical enquiry into first principles which directs a new literature as tradition guides an old one" ("Wanted-Canadian criticism": *Towards a View,* 167). Smith is against the practice of native Canadian poems evaluated in the American and English critical traditions. He writes: "Without a body of critical opinion to hearten and direct them, Canadian writers are like a leaderless army" (168). After convincing the readers about the need for a distinct Canadian critical tradition, Smith laments over the lack of unified action in this regard: "There are little skirmishes, heroic single stands: but no concerted action" (169). Finally, he puts forward a solution: "Sensibility is no longer enough, intelligence is also required. Even in Canada" (169). Smith, thus, even during his adolescence, is seen to have favoured the "poetry of ideas" to the "poetry of feeling."

After completion of his tenure at Edinburgh, Smith returned to Montreal in 1929 during severe economic depression in Canada. After a year of high school teaching, finding academic jobs scarce in Canada, he left Montreal to seek work in the United States. He received his doctoral degree in 1931. His doctoral dissertation was entitled *Studies in the Metaphysical Poets of the Anglican Church in the Seventeenth Century*. During the next several years he held short-term jobs in various American schools and colleges. Finally, in 1936, he secured a teaching appointment in the Michigan State University where he remained for 36 years until his retirement in 1972.

In the same year, jointly with F.R. Scott, he published *New Provinces*, the first anthology of modern Canadian poetry. Its publication history is quite interesting. Smith, Scott, Klein and Kennedy – the "Montreal Group" – were preparing for the publication of *New Provinces*. E.J. Pratt and Robert Finch, two Toronto poets, were eventually added, although Smith's preference was for Dorothy Livesay and W.W.E. Ross who interested him by their imagist practices.

Smith wrote for the anthology a caustic and confrontational preface in which he built up an argument on the model of "Wanted-Canadian Criticism." He wrote in this Preface: "Poetry today is written for the most part by people whose emotional and intellectual heritage is not a national one; it is either cosmopolitan or provincial, and for good or evil, the forces of civilization are rapidly making the latter scarce." ("A Rejected Preface": *Towards a View,* 170). He further added: "The fundamental criticism that must be brought against Canadian poetry as a whole is that it ignores the intelligence. And as a result it is dead" (172).

With youthful explosiveness, Smith preceded these remarks with a rigid attack on earlier Canadian poets, including in his condemnation, though he did not name them, leading poets like Roberts, Lampman and D.C. Scott. Pratt and Finch felt that this Preface would produce a controversy at the expense of the volume's contents; hence the Preface was abandoned in favour of a brief anonymous Foreword by Scott. The contents of the Preface also alienated Smith from the more strident of Canadian literary nationalists. Three decades later, Smith's Preface was rescued from oblivion and published as "A Rejected Preface" in *Canadian Literature*. Ever since, the Preface is popular in critical circles. To read that Preface now is to "realize the passion of Smith's early militancy and to understand the spirit in which he undertook to redefine and redirect the Canadian poetic tradition" (Francis, 303).

The poems in *New Provinces* had an impact on Canadian verse far beyond the controversial prefatory pronouncements. Five of Smith's frequently anthologized poems – "The Lonely Land," "The Creek," "News of the Phoenix," "Proud Parable" and "The Two Sides of a Drum" – were included in the volume. W.E. Collin, reviewing the poems in his article "Difficult, Lonely Music," observed the influence of the metaphysical poets, T.S. Eliot, the later poems of W.B. Yeats, the Grail legend and the poetry of Edith Sitwell on these poems. Collin's favourable review raised Smith to the rank of a reputed modern Canadian poet.

Though Smith was in the United States, he lost none of his interest in Canadian poetry. He came to Canada too often to relax at his summer home and to teach at summer schools in Canadian universities. In 1941, Smith obtained a Guggenheim Fellowship to prepare a historical and critical anthology of Canadian poetry. This anthology, *The Book of Canadian Poetry,* was published in 1943. It became a kind of national text-book fixing the taste of younger poets and encouraging the wider reading of poetry in Canada. Smith, by now, had mellowed down in his opinion of his contemporary poets and had added in this volume, poems by pre-modernist Canadian poets whom he ignored earlier.

In the preface to this anthology, Smith warns about colonialism as a threat to Canadian literature. He distinguishes between "cosmopolitan" and "native" verse. For him, the "cosmopolitan" poet responded to what Canadian life "had in common with life everywhere," while the "native" poet "concentrated on what is individual and unique in Canadian life." Smith saw the "native" poet as trying to "come to terms with an environment that is only now ceasing to be colonial"; the "cosmopolitan" writer, on the other hand, "from the very beginning has made a heroic effort to transcend colonialism by entering into the universal, civilizing culture of ideas" (*The Book of Canadian Poetry,* i-ix).

John Sutherland was critical of the native-cosmopolitan distinction of Smith. He made a taunting remark in "Mr. Smith and the 'Tradition'" which was appended as "Introduction" to his own anthology, *Other Canadians.* Sutherland wrote:

> "At the back of Mr. Smith's mind, there is no doubt that, the 'cosmopolitan' is the only tradition of Canadian poetry: that it is the direction in which the future is tending as well as the established fact of the past" (8).

Sutherland argued that the invention of native tradition is only a devil summoned by Smith to frighten away the adversaries of his cosmopolitanism. Almost half-a-century later in1990 when Philip Kokotailo suggested "harmonization" of Smith's native and cosmopolitan traditions into a single modern tradition, he almost promoted the opinion of Sutherland. Kokotailo wrote:

> Native and cosmopolitan impulses are not mutually exclusive, they can co-exist not only within the same mind but also within the same poem. (34).

Smith's experience in the project to publish *The Book of Canadian Poetry* made him to shed some of his erstwhile harsher judgements. Three such occasions are narrated here. The first occasion was in 1947 when *Northern Review* was created as a result of the realignment of the *New Provinces* poets with the *First Statement* group. From the beginning there had been tension between the two constituent groups. Smith tells Heenan his opinion of the *First Statement* group:

> The general difference was that the *First Statement* group were poets of 'social significance' and I had no use for that. I wanted metaphysical poetry, intellectual poetry and, perhaps, 'pure' poetry, and I think that poets like Patrick Anderson, P.K. Page and myself were poets of that sort in contrast to the *First Statement* people. Souster and Dudek and the early Layton, their hearts were in the right place all right but it seemed to me that their poetry was flat and prosaic – journalism rather than poetry. (Heenan: online)

The matter came to a head when Sutherland from the *First Statement* group wrote an aggressive article attacking the granting of a Governor-General's award to Robert Finch for his first book, *Poems* (1946). Smith rallied around Finch in this controversy and resigned from the editorial board of the magazine. By giving his support to Finch, the most conservative among the New Provinces poets, Smith had reconciled to himself and admitted his links to a tradition of pre-modernist Canadian poets.

On another occasion, Smith recognized the validity of the special kind of cosmopolitanism the Confederation poets represented, for the essay he contributed to the first issue of *Canadian Literature* in 1959 was a very deep study of the poetry of D.C. Scott.

The third occasion was in 1973 when Smith published his collection of critical essays, *Towards a View of Canadian Letters*. He devoted a substantial part of the book to the study of the Confederation poets with the ironic title "Poets of a Golden Age?"

Evidently, Smith who had been neglecting tradition in the formation of his poetic theories in his earlier career has now reconciled himself to tradition and has drawn inspiration from it. He has at last found modernism to be thriving out of tradition.

Smith's first collection of poems, *News of the Phoenix*, was published in 1943. Dorothy Livesay, reviewing the volume, considers Smith's themes "intimate and intellectually exciting," style "flawless," but indicts him for "lack of range, absence of rhetoric" (18-19). J.M. Brinin, while admiring Smith's controlled irony, chides his "inability to vitalize his images" (158), resulting in mythological clichés.

His second collection of poems, *A Sort of Ecstasy*, appeared in 1954. This collection included revised versions of thirteen poems found in the earlier volume along with twenty new poems. Desmond Pacey while reviewing the volume in *The Fiddlehead* finds Smith excelling in three types of poems: landscape description, ironic social commentary and love lyrics. Pacey declares Smith as the leading Canadian poet of his generation whose highly distilled poems "are polished gems which can be handled again and again without dulling their lustre" (*Creative Writing in Canada,* 126).

During the late 1950s, with the collapse of high modernism in Europe and America, Smith's concept of poetry was losing favour among Canadian poets. Poets like Layton, Souster and Dudek did not value Smith's poetry of "cosmopolitanism" but wrote another sort of native poetry which was "racy and vigorous," "healthy and masculine." Smith now played an important role as an anthologist becoming one of those who helped to shape the Canadian literary canon. Eli Mandel praises Smith as an anthologist arguing that "the process of selection was in itself a kind of literary criticism in which Smith excelled" ("Masks of Criticism", 24).

In the 1960s, forced by circumstances and accommodating himself to the changes, Smith formulated his concept of "eclectic detachment." He recommended this "eclectic detachment" as the appropriate stance for Canadian poets and substituted "universal" for "cosmopolitan" values, in his introduction to *The Oxford Book of Canadian Verse* (1960). However, he was again challenged. Louis Dudek, for example, suggested that true universality emerged from "a local pride." In 1967, Dudek and Michael Gnarowski compiled a historical anthology of criticism, *The Making of Modern Poetry in Canada*, which favoured a tradition of social realism. The younger poets who had emerged in that decade had passed beyond modernism into a more democratic, pluralistic, existential, and experimental mode of creativity. They were not attuned to Smith's values, nor could he respond to them sympathetically as a critic.

From then onwards, Smith began to be evaluated not as a contemporary influence but as a poetic legacy. The publication of the third collection of Smith, *Collected Poems*, in 1962 was uneventful. It was neither appreciated nor disapproved. Every time interest slackened on Smith, critics tended to present a revisionist view of him. Thoughtfully, Smith's admirers brought out a special number of *Canadian Literature* in 1963 to honour Smith for scoring hundred – for having published a hundred poems. George Woodcock, Earle Birney, Roy Fuller and Milton Wilson contributed articles. This venture helped to divert stereotyped critical attention focusing on the classical and metaphysical qualities of Smith to his energetic and life-affirming qualities. Peter Hughes praises Smith abundantly for freshness of his imagery. George Woodcock appreciates Smith's lyrical qualities and explains his interest in parody and pastiche as an indication of not of lack of invention but "a sublime form of literary criticism" ("Smith's Hundred", 3).

Smith's fourth collection of poems, *Poems: New and Collected*, appeared in 1967. After a lull of activity for about ten years, a symposium held at Michigan State University in 1976 brought Smith back to focus. Sandra Djwa, Leon Edel, M.L. Rosenthal and Eli Mandel presented papers gathering fresh insights on the classical and metaphysical qualities of Smith. In her article, "Of Metaphysics and Dry Bones," Djwa claims Smith to be a modern or neo-Metaphysical poet. She makes this claim on the basis of the metaphysical texture and the subject-matter of key-poems of Smith. She states that Smith applied neo-Platonic philosophy to the twentieth century and redefined some of the older religious concepts. She is of the opinion that Smith's dazzling poetic craftsmanship has not been given sustained consideration. His stronger poetic and critical impulse works in terms of pairs of opposites through the technique of paradox and hyperbole. Djwa's re-evaluation of Smith generated renewed interest in him.

Smith retired from Michigan State University in 1972. After his wife Jeannie died in 1977, his health declined rapidly. His fifth and final volume of poetry, *The Classical Shade*, was published in 1978. It made a very inconsequential ripple in the literary waters of Canada. After prolonged illness, Smith died on 21 November 1980 in East Lansing, Michigan.

The freezing interest in Smith was warmed up again by a special posthumous issue of *Canadian Poetry* in 1982. It included memoirs by F.R. Scott and Leon Edel. An article by D.M.R. Bentley, "Not of Things Only, but of Thought" makes a fresh stylistic analysis of Smith's imagist poems. The imagist poems are again analyzed by Anne Compton in 1989, where the author highlights the new insights that Smith had added to the imagism of T.E. Hulme.

Smith exhibits a wide range of styles and themes in his poems. His versatility has often proved a hindrance to critics seeking unity of tone and purpose in his poetry. The earliest of Smith's poems to gain recognition were heavily indebted to Yeats and Eliot. "The Lonely Land" and "Like an Old Proud King in a Parable" are the most anthologized poems of this period. "The Lonely Land" is widely admired for its precise evocation of the Canadian North. "Proud Parable" is expressive of the conflicting romantic-modernist sensibility in the poet. During the middle period of his career, in the 1930s, Smith, like most of his contemporaries, turned to poetry that dealt with social and political issues. Here he reminds us of the Pylon poets Auden and Day Lewis. "News of the Phoenix" is the best example of his satirical poems; its double edged irony is remarkable. In two other poems of this period, "Far West" and "Noctambule," Smith is very complex, demanding the reader's ability to identify and appreciate a wide range of allusions that underlie an apparently surreal vision. These works give credence to Smith's metaphysical qualities, not only in their juxtaposition of seemingly unrelated images but also in their fusion of intellect and feeling, abstract ideas and human emotions.

In his later poetry, Smith dwells increasingly on the theme of death. His awareness of the inevitability of death produces defiant rejection of death as in the poems of Tennyson and Emily Dickinson and in Shakespeare's *Romeo and Juliet* and *Antony and Cleopatra*. Two poems of this period, "Metamorphosis" and "The Wisdom of Old Jelly Roll," with images of sensuality and regeneration, highlight Smith's unshakeable commitment to life. The same theme is most lovingly and dynamically explored in "The Archer," considered his finest poem by many.

It would be a fallacy, however, to place Smith entirely in the modernistic tradition. In the symposium held at Michigan State University in 1976, Rosenthal and Sandra Djwa have emphasized that Smith's eclectic modernism is balanced by an equally strong pull towards romanticism. Rosenthal writes: "In the Romantic-Classic debate, Smith tends to vote classical on principle while his poems actually throw the balance of feeling and imagination a little the other way" ("Poor Innocent", 13). Sandra Djwa has also noted this dual orientation. She writes: "A romantic at heart he responded to the general post-war disillusionment and to the particular circumstances of his own career with a cultivated irony . . . characteristic of modernism" ("Of Metaphysics and Dry Bones", 33). In another article, she rightly justifies this modern-romantic syncretism: "In Canada, [as in some of the east European countries] where romanticism came late and where the introduction of modernism coincided with the revival of the national spirit, the modern was also the buoyantly romantic ("A New Soil and a Sharp Sun", 34).

The contradictory desire to embrace a lush romantic loveliness and to purge oneself of it in lonely austerity is a repeated theme in many of Smith's poems. This dual structure which seems to have emerged naturally from his British background and the influence of Yeats, is reflected in his approach to modern Canadian poetry. His modernism is at least in part a reaction against his romantic self.

This book makes a detailed study of Smith's modernism and his "divided sensibility," to borrow a phrase from Michael Darling. It makes an in-depth analysis of about 50 poems of

Smith focusing on the romantic-classic diffusions. Smith has published about 200 poems. While selecting poems for analysis, greater attention was paid to those poems which have been frequently anthologized and those which have drawn much critical attention. A list of Smith's published poems with first-publication details is appended to this book.

2

A Meadow in the Northern Stone: Smith's Lapidary Poems

In his early career Smith wrote "lapidary" verse – scrupulously planned, carefully chiselled out, high fidelity *object d'art*. But the more perfect these verses were, much glaring was the romantic-modernist conflict in them. The fluctuation between a sensuous, life-affirming romanticism ("meadow") and an austere, timeless classicism ("northern stone") is a recurrent motif in these poems. Smith's recent readings of Yeats and the metaphysical poets were fresh in him that there is a fecund freshness in the poems of this period. In all the poems, the romantic-modern dichotomy is noticeable. In some of the poems, there is an undercurrent of uncertainty and disillusionment.

Vain Comfort (1925)

"Vain Comfort" is an instinctive youthful poem exhibiting a romantic sensibility. Smith was influenced by Yeats to write this poem. Critics compare "Vain Comfort" with Yeats's Maud Gonne poems like "The Folly of Being Comforted" (1902) and "Old Memory" (1904). The Yeats of the Celtic Twilight was an irresistible influence on the young Smith. In his MA thesis, Smith claims that Yeats was concerned "wholly and completely with the devout passion of love, and the quest of ideal loveliness" (3). The following lines from the poem express the poet's painful awareness of fading beauty:

> All dear sweet things grow gray;
> Time steals the fire from eyes,

And cracks clear laughter's bell,
Making of truths sad lies,
Changing felicities
To memories.

Yeats's influence apart, there are many such familiar descriptions of withering beauty in the English language, particularly in the Elizabethan sonnet tradition and in the romantic poetry of Keats. Shakespeare, in a mood of nostalgic dreaminess, writes in one of his sonnets on the ephemeral nature of time and beauty:

When to the sessions of sweet silent thought
I summon up remembrance of things past,
I sigh the lack of many a things I sought,
And with old woes new wail my dear time's waste.

Keats writes in his "Lines of Fancy":

Everything is spoilt by use:
Where's the cheek that doth not fade,
Too much gaz'd at? Where's the maid
Whose lip mature is ever new?
Where's the eye, however blue,
Doth not weary?

The typical sensuousness of Keats in the lines "Where's the eye, however blue, / Doth not weary?" is characteristically represented by Smith in the line "Time steals the fire from eyes." Louis Dudek rightly remarks that Smith's aesthetic vision is a "combination of Keats and Baudelaire" ("A Load of New Books", 169). Obviously the content of "Vain Comfort" is romantic and the mood austere.

Prayer (1925)

Smith wrote "Prayer" only two months after "Vain Comfort." It is strange that the two poems represent opposite tones. Smith describes his artistic credo and the subsequent conflict in the poem. In the last stanza of the poem, Smith pleads to God to give him the mind to hold in a poem the spirit of "prairie and river" (romantic) and the austerity of "dear / The North" (modernism):

> To hold in a verse as austere
> As the spirit of prairie and river,
> Lonely unbuyable, dear
> The North, as a deed, and forever.

The poem manifests Smith's conflicting desire to hold a lush romantic loneliness and to purge himself of it in lonely austerity.

Like an Old Proud King in a Parable (1926)

One of Smith's very popular poems, "Like an Old Proud King in a Parable," first appeared in *McGill Fortnightly Review* in 1926. It was revised and published in *Canadian Mercury* in 1928; again revised and published in *Hound and Horn* in1932 with the addition of the important tenth line, "O who is that bitter king? It is not I," and the last three lines. In this poem, a king renounces his throne to become a poet and sing "difficult, lonely music." At one level, the poem is a perfect example of Smith's determination to turn his back on the world and lead an austere, hard, lonely life. At another level, the poem is symbolic of Smith's ambivalent sensibility to the romantic-modernist split. The aggressive flinging away of robe and responsibilities is, in symbolic terms, a stripping away of florid diction and overwrought emotions. A confrontation with the inner self is suggested by the poet's renunciation of any audience but the barren rock.

The farewell imagery in the first five lines of the poem is poignant:

> A bitter king in anger to be gone
> From fawning courtier and doting queen
> Flung hollow sceptre and gilt crown away,
> And breaking bound of all his countries green
> He made a meadow in the northern stone.

The words "bitter," "anger" and "flung" are signifiers of intense feelings. The king is compelled to sacrifice certain things which he never wanted to sacrifice, hence the use of these words of anguish, anger and unwillingness. The king is not only unwilling to sacrifice the existing comforts but also hesitant to go to the place where he finally has to go, "the northern stone." "Stone" is symbolic of hardness, rigidity and austerity; "northern stone" because northern part of Canada is cold, rugged and barren. These five lines can be summarized in a sentence: a king is hesitant to forego the pleasures of the kingdom to lead the life of an austere poet. The implied meaning is that Smith is unwilling to swap romanticism with modernism. The emotion-charged words and phrases in the above lines and the words of rigidity and loneliness – "inviolable," "cage," "alone" and "pride" – in the lines that follow justify this viewpoint:

> And breathed a palace of inviolable air
> To cage a heart that carolled like a swan
> And slept alone, immaculate and gay
> With only his pride for a paramour.

The King's divesting of kingship reminds us of a similar situation in Tennyson's poem "Ulysses." Tennyson found Ulysses an apt inter-text to showcase the philistinism and provincialism of the Victorian people. He exemplifies in the poem the conflicting Victorian sensibility of admiration for new knowledge and scientific development on the one hand, and the attitude of withdrawal from a life of development and materialism on the other. In Tennyson's poem, King Ulysses returns to his kingdom Ithaca after the Trojan War. But all is bad in Ithaca. His domestic bliss is disturbed. He is bewildered. He wants to renounce kingship, escape reality, and go on a voyage and "drink / Life to the lees." Ulysses voices his anguish in a self-mocking ironic tone. The poem is replete with verses like,

> . . . gray spirit yearning in desire
> To follow knowledge like a sinking star.

and

> . . . my purpose holds
> To sail beyond the sunset and the baths
> Of all the western stars, until I die.

until, finally, the poem ends in a peak of paradox:

> To strive, to seek, to find, and not to yield.

This concluding line shows the poet Tennyson's self-mocking desire to fight against the "development" during the Victorian era. This conflict keeps raging in him inconclusively.

The same kind of conflict exists in Smith. But his feelings are antithetical to that of Tennyson. Tennyson is happy to flee the disappointing present. Smith is disappointed to give away the happy present. These opening lines of "Ulysses" need to be compared with that of "Proud Parable":

> It little profits that an idle king,
> By this still hearth, among these barren crags,
> Matched with an aged wife, I mete and dole
> Unequal laws into a savage race
> That hoard and sleep, and feed and know not me.

Tennyson's Ulysses is happy to flee his kingdom because he will miss only an "aged wife" (miserable domestic life), a "savage race" (uncivilized citizens) and "barren crags" (unfertile country). Smith's king is unhappy to cross boundaries of his kingdom because he will miss a "doting queen" (happy familial life), "fawning courtier" (obedient citizens) and "countries green" (fertile country).

In Smith's poem, the desire to abdicate in the first nine lines quoted above is undercut by an intruding tenth line: "O who is that bitter king? It is not I." This line was not found in the poem in 1926 but was later added in 1932. Among other changes in the poem, Smith eliminated the phrase "blood and bone" and his weakness for apostrophe – "O kingly One!" – and created the memorable "difficult, lonely music" which has become a catch-phrase for his poetry. These revisions indicate very important conceptual changes in Smith's modernism during the intermittent years between the first and subsequent publications of the poem. The trend in such verbal revisions is "the elimination of hackneyed romantic diction and the substitution of vivid images" (Michael Darling: "A.J.M. Smith's revision to His Poems", 11).

By introducing the above-mentioned tenth interrupting line, Smith wants to ensure that he is not identified with the austere king in the poem. It is a dislocating device employed by him to depersonalize the poem. This line is intended to severe the kinship between the speaker of the poem (king) and the poet. Having done this, the king now conjoins his hands and prays to the Lord, the Father, beseeching him to make his difficult heart to cooperate:

> Let me, I beseech thee, Father, die
> From this fat royal life, and lie
> As naked as a bridegroom by his bride
> And let that girl be the cold goddess Pride.

These lines bring to our mind Yeats's similar plea in "Sailing to Byzantium":

> O sages . . .
> Consume my heart away; sick with desire
> And fastened to a dying animal
> It knows not what it is; and gather me
> Into the artifice of eternity.

"Proud Parable" ends in a typical note of self-mockery, like the concluding line of "Ulysses," as the unrobed king prays to be able to learn a superior, isolated art:

> And I will sing to the barren rock
> Your difficult, lonely music, heart,
> Like an old proud king in a parable.

The king's renunciation of any audience but the barren rock suggests a confrontation with the inner-self.

Testament (1927)

In "Testament" Smith declares his intention to give up this worldly life and seek a godly world. The poem opens with a rhetorical flourish:

> I'm for the desert and the desolation.

In the lines that follow, Smith announces his intention to give up this worldly life:

> I have kissed my hands to distant trees
> And to the girls with pitchers
> Waiting at the well –

But what is the alternative? Where is he proceeding to? His reply is:

> And I am set upon a pilgrimage
> Seeking a more difficult beauty
> Unheartened by even the most faint mirage.

Smith wants to give up this worldly life and seek communion with God, though the words "difficult," "unheartened" and "faint" suggest that the wish may not be achieved. Meanwhile, the crescendo built up earlier reaches its climax in the final line:

> I am not I, but a generation

It is not Smith's wish alone to seek communion but that of all the people of the world. Thus, there is, in the poem, a progression of feeling from personal to universal. "When Smith composes poems with a strong personal intent, he sees himself in relation to a continuing tradition, an [ironic] attitude, which keeps the personal element confined and yet achieves a kind of enlargement for it by identifying it with a larger entity" (Nageswara Rao, 117).

Apart from its religious overtones, like "Proud Parable," "Testament" is also a poem concerned with poetry and the nature of the poetic process. Smith's farewell "to distant trees / And to the girls with pitchers" is likened to a farewell to his hitherto florid diction and romantic musings. The "pilgrimage" refers to his laborious journey towards classicism, "a difficult beauty" but it is also "the blood and body of our unknown God." Nothing would stop him, not the "most faint mirage" or "the grey and yellow desert stone." The atmosphere of self-mockery in "Proud Parable" is repeated here.

"Proud Parable" and "Testament" are two very important poems in the Smith canon which have evoked much criticism and have been subjected to many interpretations. When first published, these were personal poems expressing romantic and religious sentiments respectively. But in the following years, after Smith had established himself as a modernist, he made many revisions to eliminate subjectivity from these poems, called depersonalization revision in critical circles. In spite of these revisions and depersonalization through modernistic techniques, the romantic elements are strikingly apparent in these poems.

Beside One Dead (1927)

"Beside One Dead" is a companion poem of "Testament." In this poem, Smith makes a philosophical argument through a religious myth:

> This is the sheath,
> the sword drawn,
> These are the lips,
> the word spoken,
> This is Calvary
> toward dawn
> And this is the
> third-day token –
> The opened tomb
> and the Lord gone
> Something whole
> that was broken.

The poem hints at the liturgical drama performed in the middle of the tenth century, called the *Quem Quaeritis,* in which the three Marys seeking the entombed Christ find his sepulchre empty; an angel appears to them and tells them of his resurrection; cheerful over the tidings they turn toward the choir and the congregation breaks into a ritual of prayer *Te Deum Laudamus.* Eliot's pageant "The Rock" too ends in a ceremonial prayer that sweeps the audience into an act of worship. Similarly, *Murder in the Cathedral* ends in a *Te Deum* as in some mediaeval plays. But Smith's poem is different. It treats the idea of how the soul, while it is still in the body, partakes of certain privations of life and yearns for union with God. But underneath this superficial structure there are specific images of loss, absence and incompletion: the sword drawn from the sheath, disembodied lips, the opened tomb, the Lord absent, the dissipated whole. And there is no sense of a speaker to confirm the faith. Smith presents, in this poem, a disintegrated religious scene in a subtle manner. The resolution and faith achieved in Eliot and the mediaeval plays is absent in Smith.

Shadows There Are (1927)

The poem is a sandwich-poem with a couplet squeezed between two three-line stanzas with similar rhyme schemes. The really classical poet and the really romantic poet are at work in this poem:

> Shadows there are, but shadows such as these
> Are shadows only in the mortal mind,
> Blown by the spirit or the spirit's wind.
>
> Yet shadows I have seen, of me deemed deeper,
> That backed on nothing in the horrid air,
>
> And try as try, I cannot limn the form
> That some of them assume where I shall pass.
> They grow transparent, and as sharp, as glass.

The three stanzas are like three distorted mirrors. They play with the idea of shadow and form in a way that suggests the mind's bafflement when confronting its own limitations. The ambiguity here is true to the lyric tradition. Smith reaches back to Elizabethan poets who flung a mood at the mercy of the language and thereby discovered that the mood was a world of involvement.

The ambiguous pronoun "these" in the first line of the poem stands for a set of perceptions or ideas that is never precisely explained. The speaker attempts to discriminate between two kinds of shadows, one comprehended by the mind and the other by the senses: "shadows I have seen." The really "seen" shadows frustrate the speaker's attempts to determine and describe the unseen, illusionary shadows. These shadows become ominous ("as sharp as glass") as they grow less visible and "these" unknown, mysterious shadows are the ones to be feared the most.

The poem has a complex structure with the inversion of syntax as in the title "Shadows There Are" and in the couplet "Yet shadows I have seen, of me deemed deeper," and the unusual phrase, "try as try." The speaker says that he cannot draw or paint ("I cannot limn the form") the shapes that some of the shadows assume in his mind. It is this enduring sense of the shapeless beyond shape which gives Smith's poems the sense of austerity.

"Shadows There Are" demonstrates Smith's modernism, which is not merely a demand for superficially formal tightness, but a serious philosophical pursuit of the implications of contemporary mentality and sensibility.

A Hyacinth for Edith (1927)

"A Hyacinth for Edith" shows Smith's growing interest in parody. The poem is a parody of the English poet Edith Sitwell. A parody can be defined as imitation "turned as to produce a ridiculous effect." A parody, in general usage, is a work created to mock or comment on the original work, its subject, author or style by means of humorous, satiric or ironic imitation. *Mac Flecknoe* by John Dryden and *Joseph Andrews* by Henry Fielding are examples.

However, in ancient Greek literature, a *parodia* was a narrative poem imitating the style and prosody of epics. In the broader sense of Greek *parodia*, parody can occur when whole elements of one work are lifted out of their context and reused, not necessarily to be ridiculed. The literary theorist Linda Hutcheon argues that this Greek sense of parody has again become prevalent in the twentieth century, as writers have sought to connect with the past while registering differences brought by modernity. As Linda Hutcheon puts it, "parody . . . is imitation, not always at the expense of the parodied text" (7). Another critic, Simon Dentith, defines parody as "any cultural practice which provides a relatively polemical allusive imitation of another cultural production or practice" (9). Such a parody in which a writer takes the basic form of a text and places it in a new context without ridiculing it is called Blank Parody. A modernist example of this blank or re-contextualizing parody is James Joyce's *Ulysses*.

In "A Hyacinth for Edith," Smith makes a blank or re-contextualizing parody of Edith. Edith Sitwell (1887-1964) was an ardent proponent of modernism. Her early work reflected the strong influence of the French symbolists. She edited *Wheels,* an annual anthology of modern verse. She published a number of volumes of verse in which she exploited the musical qualities of language. She published a poem, *Gold Coast Customs*, in the rhythms of the tom-tom and of jazz, and showed considerable technical skill. In 1922 she published *Façade* a series of abstract poems the rhythms of which counterfeited those of music. In the same year Eliot published *The Waste Land.* In the furious controversy that raged in the press throughout the 1920s, Eliot and Sitwell were popularly perceived as marching "hand in hand . . . in the vanguard of modernism." Together the two had polarized public opinion still further between the "ancients" and the "moderns." Smith makes use of Sitwell's current popularity to write a poem on her. His poem "A Hyacinth for Edith" is a show of solidarity with Sitwell on her commitment to modernism. And it moves beyond parody to stand as a commentary on the times, prefiguring Smith's war-time satires.

In his book *The Language of Humour,* Walter Nash explains how the parodic intent can be recognized in a poem: "The reader is given some form of stylistic proposition, a poet's name is mentioned and content is indicated" (88). In "A Hyacinth for Edith," Edith's name is mentioned in the title. It is well known that Edith exploited the musical qualities of language in her poem *Gold Coast Customs* and the *Façade* poems. "A Hyacinth" with its alliterative rhyming lines has a musical rhythm. Smith employs in the poem a technique familiarized by Edith – the description of one kind of sense experience in terms of another: "clacking" of "ashen rain" describes sight in terms of sound. Nash's requirement of stylistic proposition is thus fulfilled in the poem.

"A Hyacinth for Edith," when first published in 1927, it was in the manner of parody of Edith Sitwell's Troy Park poems. However, when revised and published in 1930, it moved beyond parody to stand as a commentary on the times anticipating Smith's social satires of the thirties and forties.

The poem is in 13 couplets of 26 lines. In the first four couplets there is a familiar description of the spring:

> Now that the ashen rain of gummy April
> Clacks like a weedy and stain'd mill,
>
> So that all the tall purple trees
> Are pied porpoises in swishing seas.
>
> And the yellow horses and milch cows
> Come out of their long frosty house
>
> To gape at the straining flags
> The brown pompous hill wags.

In this depressive description of spring there are plenty of colour images: "purple trees," "yellow horses" and "brown pompous hill." This gloomy description of April rain takes us to a similar situation in Keats's *The Ode to Melancholy:*

> But when the melancholy fit shall fall
> Sudden from heaven like a weeping cloud,
> That fosters the drooping-headed flowers all
> And hides the green hill in an April shroud;
> Then glut the sorrow on a morning rose.

Keats describes the bleak "weeping cloud" fostering the drooping flowers and watering the green hills; Smith describes the "ashen rain of gummy April" bending the whooshing pines towards the swishing sea. Keats's picture is that of the April showers on the English countryside; Smith's representation is that of the spring rains on the cold Canadian coast. Both depictions are evocative, only the landscapes are different.

The fifth stanza is shifty in many ways. The colour imagery ends; the down-sliding purple, yellow and brown colours of the earlier couplets terminate in black. Observation shifts to reflection. The poet declares an intense wish:

> I'll seek within the woods' black plinth
> A Candy-sweet sleek wooden hyacinth –

The next two couplets drown the speaker in a reverie:

> And in its creaking naked glaze,
> And in the varnish of its blaze,
>
> The bird of ecstasy shall sing again.
> The bearded sun shall spring again,

A few couplets later, the reverie shifts from the description of verdant nature ("naked glaze") to the scenes of city-life and its fake realities ("tinsel paradise") and lost joy:

> Lurking within this tinsel paradise
> Of trams and cinemas and manufactured ice
>
> Till I am grown again my own lost ghost
> Of joy, long lost, long given up for lost.

Finally, the meaningless, contemporary world is left behind and the speaker longs for the innocent, beautiful world of childhood:

> And walk again the wild and sweet wildwood
> Of our lost innocence, our ghostly childhood.

The poem has a shifting pattern of romantic and realistic images. Beginning with the familiar April reference, Smith has structured the poem in terms of the hyacinth myth of *The Waste Land*. But here it is the contemplation of the wooden hyacinth— the artefact of the imagination – which might restore the waste land of the trivial present. The poem has a reality – illusion – disillusion – restoration sequence. It begins with a description of the disappointments of the present, followed by a ray of hope in the middle, and the concluding lines describe a longing for return to childhood pleasures. A similar desire to return to the innocent world of childhood to escape from the ravages of war is the subject matter of another of Smith's poem, "Ode: The Eumenides," which he wrote in 1941.

Eden's Isle (1957)

Though written 30 years after "Beside One Dead," the theme of loss and absence in "Beside One Dead" is continued in "Eden's Isle." It is an allusive poem. It alludes to Shakespeare's *The Tempest,* and the poem contrasts the joyful disposition of Caliban in an unknown island with the "querulous" nature of the modern man in a known island. In *The Tempest,* Caliban soothes Stephano not to be scared of the strange noises of the island. He tells him that they are sweet and sober enough to charm a man to slumber and will never hurt:

> Be not afeard: the isle is full of noises,
> Sounds and sweet airs, that give delight, and hurt
> not.
> Sometimes a thousand twangling instruments
> Will hum about mine ears; and sometimes voices,
> That, if I then had wak'd after long sleep
> Will make me sleep again. (3.2. 132-37)

But, in Smith's Eden, contemporary people, the descendents of Caliban, hear "yelping voices," and "heavier roar":

> 'The Isle is full of noises.'
> The sea runs at the shore
> With querulous yelping voices
> And a hollow, heavier roar.

The sea is an archetypal symbol for strength, power and purity; but where the sea meets the land it becomes irritable ("The sea runs at the shore / With querulous yelping voices"). Matthew Arnold had a similar experience on the shores of the Dover Beach ("Where the sea meets the moon-blanched land, / Listen! You hear the grating roar"). Arnold and Smith had deep concern for social and moral issues of the world and are shocked at the loss of these values due to the materialism of the contemporary people. The next stanza reads:

> The sea wind in the oak trees
> Shrieks like a prophet of death
> Or whines as a man will wheeze
> Who fights for his last breath.

The sea wind "whines" and "wheezes" like an asthmatic man struggling for his breath. In the first two stanzas, Smith is, thus, contemplating the chaotic nature of the world of water when it meets the earth. The third stanza extends the imagery of death and relates it to the crumbling of cliffs and the mooring of vessels – the chaos on earth:

> The cliffs crumble to chalk
> Where the breakers thunder and thud
> The vessels moored at the dock
> Are drained of their life blood.

"Cliffs," "vessels" and "dock" allude to the material world and the words "crumble," "thud" and "drain" are expressive of destruction. The reference to the eagle in the last stanza takes the readers to the world of space. The focus shifts from sound to visual images. The stanza reads:

> The eagle rides on the storm:
> His shadow blots out the Isle:
> And in the East, the immovable form
> Of the Sphinx smiles a stone smile.

The chaotic world of the earth is overpowered by the chaotic world of space. The "crumble" and the "shrieks" of the modern world are withholding human beings of their vision of Eden. In the east, the mythological Sphinx, suggestive of aridity and sterility, makes "a stone smile" at the plight of the present-day world. The image of loss of vision as the Eagle's "shadow blots out the Isle" is a reconstruction of "The opened tomb / and the Lord gone" in "Beside One Dead."

The Offices of the First and the Second Hour (1933)

Smith presents a spiritual subject in a classical perspective in this poem. It is in three parts. In the first part, Smith makes a description of a poet's first exercises in the "athleticism" or "training of the soul" (W.E. Collin 253). To create the proper atmosphere for spiritual exercise, Smith has made the poem look like a fragment of the Divine office of the Roman Church. He questions "What is the office of the first hour?" and answers that it is "To abjure":

> To abjure the kindness of darkness humbly
> To concede the irrelevant spite of the spirit,
> The night-like melancholy flesh-case and the
> Romantic unnecessary cape of the naked heart.

Here darkness is described as kind and humble because it acts unseen and without restraint. The inference is that, at the first stage, careless ways and unnecessary romanticism of the naked heart must be regarded as irrelevant to real spiritual life. Smith calls a human being a "manlike shape" and an "articulate mandrake." The vanity of human beings is drained out slowly as a result of the spiritual discipline of the first hour. "And what is the office of the second hour?" The answer is:

> Quietly to attend the unfolding light's stark,
> Patience, inhuman and faithful like a weed or a flower,
> Empty of darkness and light.

At the second stage, which is "empty of darkness" one needs to wait quietly and in patience for the unfolding of the light of truth and grace.

In this poem, Smith has dealt with two modes of living: those who live by the flesh who are materialists and those who live by the spirit who are spiritualists. The poem may be regarded as Smith's *Divine Comedy* in order to show ho v this poem is classical in reference (Nageswara Rao, 127). The poem is in three units corresponding to the three phases in *Divine Comedy*. In the first, we see the malevolence and malice of the human heart. This part may be compared to Dante's "inferno." The second part of the poem where all the sins and sufferings of the humankind are pardoned may be compared to "purgatio." And in the third part where Smith talks of the reach of light may be related to Dante's "paradiso."

To the Christian Doctors (1936)

Smith's Neo-Platonic ideas are manifest in this poem. It is a sonnet which argues against the Christian or Platonic insistence on the superiority of the spirit over the flesh. The first three lines of the octave read:

> Send not the innocent heart to find
> In civil tears denials of the blood
> Or in humility feign kinglihood.

The octave sets out an argument where it is suggested that a civil war is waged in the body where the spirit ("innocent heart") is set against the demands of the body ("blood"). This assumption of superiority of the heart accompanied by a false humility ("in humility feign kinglihood") would:

> . . . filch his character away and bind
> Him spiritless, whom Holiness designed,
> To swell the vein with a secular flood.

Spirit, in this context, is a carefully contrived pun. Firstly, it is the courageous spirit of the heart. Secondly, it is an allusion to the animal spirits carried by the blood. Thirdly, it refers to the Holy Spirit. In this poem, as in Neo-Platonic philosophy, "the heavenly bodies affect the soul of man through the medium of air, so soul touches soul through the medium of body" (Sandra Djwa, "Of Metaphysics and Dry Bones", 28). In Smith's metaphor, the sexual impulse is:

> . . . a secular flood
> In pure ferocious joy, efficient and good,
> Like a tiger's spring on the leap of the wind.

The spiritual is not separate from the physical but animates it. The measured beat of the penultimate line and the force of the last line provide the poetic equivalent of the ecstasy that the sonnet describes:

> Whose end it is to burn sensation's lode,
> With animal intensity, to Mind.

The sonnet ends with the recognition that just as the heart cannot exist without the blood or the blood without the heart, so the spirit must animate the flesh. The sonnet form is a traditional device used by the poets to emote, the theme of the poem is philosophical, and the connotation is modern, hence the poem suggests a progression from "sense" through "blood" to "mind," an ecstasy which is both sacred and secular.

The Faithful Heart (1939)

In "The Faithful Heart," Smith presents an argument between the inner and the outer self of man, a clash between body and soul. The outer-self says:

> O Heart, I said, be silent, the world itself grows cold,
> The brave songs all are sung, the Satyrs all are old,
> And old the Principalities where once in May we went
> All garlanded with flowers who now keep narrow Lent.
> I said our sweet lord Pan, by Judas Time betrayed,
> Sleeps in the dusty tomb with Strength and Beauty laid.

This stanza describes the wavering nature of the instinct. By making use of the myth of Pan and a Christian reference to the betrayal of Christ by Judas, Smith conveys the struggle between body and soul in which the impulsive nature of man is trying to betray his faithful heart. The heart, the inner-self, responds thus:

> My true-religious heart upbraided my unfaith –
> She will not feel the frost, she'll not acknowledge death.

> She says, poor fond enthusiast, the goatfoot god is slain
> But like a god, whom we shall see rise from the tomb again.
> She quavers we shall know him as lusty as of yore
> And bear the vine-tipped thyrsus into the woods once more.

The soul wants to put an end to the instinctive drives of the heart. The "true-religious heart" is finally seen to "bear the vine-tipped thyrsus into the woods once more." In this poem, Smith exhibits his awareness of the distinction between the sacred and the sacrilege.

We have discussed some of Smith's lapidary poems on religion and metaphysics: "Testament," "Beside One Dead," "Eden's Isle," "The Offices of the First and Second Hour," "To the Christian Doctors" and "The Faithful Heart." At this point, it is relevant to debate whether Smith professed religion in his religious poems. Critics differ in their estimation. Collin, in his article "Difficult, Lonely Music" sets afloat a tradition identifying "sacramental symbolism" and "high Christian values" in Smith's poems (255). He speaks of Smith's "mystic austerity." He tells of Smith's desire to defeat "the irony of life's illusions by walking straight into the desert . . . and facing the 'difficult lonely music'" (260). Smith is named a spiritual brother of T.S. Eliot whose poetry "reflected a desire to lead a life consecrated to an austere, lonely and mystical ideal" (263). Taking his cue from Collin, John Ferns assesses Smith more as "a religious poet than as a metaphysical who grew into a secular tradition" (44).

But another school of critics favours the view that religion is secondary to Smith. These critics consider religion merely a sourcebook of imagery for him. E.K. Brown states: "Religion was a minor theme in Mr. Smith's work; it was scarcely more than an armoury of imagery . . . The main effect is that of the Bellini portrait of Christ: haggard, stricken, at odds with life" ("The Development of Poetry in Canada", 39). Desmond Pacey presents a similar view. He writes that Smith's religious poems "seem to be rather technical exercises than the product of deep religious feeling" (*Ten Canadian Poets,* 126). Similarly, Michael

Darling does not accept Smith as a religious poet. He writes in his book *Canadian Writers and Their Works*:

> His [smith's] poems . . . are unsatisfactory *as religious poetry* because they lack any sense of personal commitment, faith or honest doubt.
> Unlike Donne or Herbert, Smith does not wrestle with the concepts of sin or free will or salvation; he simply presents a Christian scene in a restrained, impersonal manner. (245)

Darling cites three sources to defend his stand that Smith was not a religious poet. Firstly, his argument: "His [Smith's] adoption of Eliot's theory of impersonal poetry and predilection for concealment behind poetic masks would dictate the unsuitability of personal religious expression to a man of Smith's temperament" (246).

Secondly, Darling cites a note by Smith himself appended to a copy of an M.A. thesis entitled "To Capture Proteus: A Study of A.J.M. Smith" where Smith makes the following remark on his "religious" poems:

> These poems are neither expressions nor illustrations of faith. They are impersonal, objective, expository – appreciative criticism, perhaps, – even appreciative parody perhaps, though I suppose neither Collin nor Miss McCullum [the candidate] could be expected to know this without being tipped off. (277)

Thirdly, Darling cites an unpublished letter which Smith wrote to Sandra Djwa in February 1976. Smith states in this letter:

> My poetic impulse may be metaphysical but not religious. All the religious elements are either scholarly and descriptive or ironic. I have written some poems, well done enough to fool people into thinking they are genuine, but they aren't. (246)

It is now obvious that Smith did not have a firm commitment to religion. Dorothy Livesay rightly identifies in him an "attitude of withdrawal." She adds, ". . . in the present mood of the world, such poetry will not give sustenance nor direction" (18). In fact, it is this lack of commitment which marks Smith off from Eliot and E.J. Pratt.

In Eliot's writings, the change from agnosticism to Christianity has a marked pattern of progress. The agony of *The Waste Land* is followed by *The Hollow Men,* with quotations from the Lord's Prayer, and *Ash Wednesday,* with its rendering of Dante's saying "In His will is our peace." Christ's saying, "Be ye therefore perfect" (Mathew V., 48), is the strength in Beckett's action and in his passion in *Murder in the Cathedral,* and in the martyrdom of Celia Coplestone in *The Cocktail Party.*

Likewise, Pratt takes up the issue of religion and moral concerns with thoughtful and mature imagination. The problem of impersonal cruelty in nature, of the conflict of species, of brute nature lurking in the heart of man, acts as a veritable unifying theme, almost an obsession, in all of Pratt's poems. His resolution of the conflict in Christianity – "The path lies through Gethsemane" – is a categorical solution very much like T.S. Eliot's categorical return to faith and religion. Such perceptible development is absent in Smith's poems on religion.

Ode on the Death of W. B. Yeats (1941)

"Ode on the Death of W. B. Yeats" is yet another *object d'art* of Smith which he wrote to commemorate Yeats. Smith's dissertation for his masters' degree was on the poetry of Yeats. Smith and Yeats had many things in common. Yeats did not take modernism very seriously, as he was very conscious of the great literary heritage of the English language. It is true that when he was in close contact with Ezra Pound, he absorbed and assimilated modernist ideas and there was a new hardness in his poems. But he never forgot to retain his conservatism. For example, he had no truck with free verse in which the modernists seemed so much at home. In the case of Smith, we are aware of the romantic-modernist split in him. He too did not indulge in free verse. He rather experimented and revised many romantic poetic forms like the ode, sonnet and elegy. Yeats was popular for his landscape patriotism. Though Ireland is a country of rude and rough landscape, Yeats zealously described it as "A terrible beauty is born" ("Easter 1916"). Smith was no less zealous in describing the dissonant beauty of Canadian northern landscape: "This is the beauty / of strength broken by strength / and still strong" ("The Lonely Land"). With such fraternal similarities, it is no wonder that Smith commemorated Yeats in a poem.

Though named an ode, the poem has all the characteristics of an elegy: Yeats's birth and life is celebrated; his death mourned; there is an expression of joy and celebration as Yeats is bestowed immortality. Then, why did Smith name it an ode? It is because an ode is an address and this poem is addressed to the people of Canada at a time they required positive energy. Smith's advice to his fellow Canadians in this poem is to be patriotic, strong and single-minded like Yeats at times of personal and national crisis. As such, Smith wrote the poem with two purposes: to remember Yeats in a poem, and implant patriotism and positivism in the readers.

The poem is in five sections. The usual conflict in Smith's poetry is evident in this poem in the imagery. In the first section, Smith describes the stormy and chaotic condition of Ireland when Yeats was born and became popular:

> An old thorn tree in a stormy place
> Where the mountain stream has run dry,
> Turn in the black wind under the race
> Of icicle sharp kaleidoscopic white sky,
> Bursts into sudden flower.

The old thorn tree, the stony place, the dry mountain stream, the black wind, and the rapidly changing sky are symbols of distress and disillusionment. But when the tree "bursts into sudden flower," it is a life-affirming situation. Yeats, Smith seems to say, has at last come like a "sudden flower" to save Ireland from the storm and chaos.

In the second section, Smith mourns the death of Yeats and describes the departure of his soul:

Under the central dome of winter and night
A wild swan spreads his fantaştic wing.
Ancestralled energy of blood and power
Beats his sinewy breast. And now the ravening
Soul, fulfilled, his first-last hour
Upon him, chooses to exult.

The soul having spent "the first-last hour upon him" is now on its flight. The soul is compared to a swan, which is a classical symbol for peace, purity and prosperity. The words "wild," "fantastic," "ancestral led energy," "blood and power" and "sinewy breast" connote life affirming qualities.

The third section describes the plummeting of the swan / soul and its flight against the storm braving the rough Irish skyscape:

Over the edge of shivering Europe
Over the chalk front of Eire, over Eire,
Dwarfing the crawling waves amoral savagery,
Daring the hiding clouds' rhetorical tumult,
The white swan plummets the mountain top.

The flight of the swan / soul brings to mind the flight of the gannet in the French Canadian novel *Shadow of the Wind* by Anne Herbert. Its flight, its headlong plunges, its struggle with the storm is of utmost interest. The fourth section is a wholesome contrast:

The stream has suddenly pushed the papery leaves!
It digs a rustling channel of clear water
On the sacred flank of Ben Bulben.
The twisted tree is incandescent with flowers,
The swan leaps singing into the cold air.

Clear water flows in the erstwhile dry stream. The flow of water has moved the dry, frail leaves. The thorn tree is bright with flowers. The swan no more leaps over shivering Europe or makes a rhetorical tumult, but flies gently into the cold air. The last, fifth section of the poem continues the rejoicing:

This is a glory not for an hour.
Over the Galway shore

The white bird is flying
Forever, and crying
To the tumultuous throng,
Of the sky his cold and passionate song.

What is gratifying is that the swan's / soul's flight is not a glory for an hour but a permanent splendour. The white bird is flying forever singing "his cold and passionate song." In functional terms, Smith celebrates Yeats's soul for having attained immortality.

The poem, being an ode, is short with well-organized strophes. The poem is important because it expresses Smith's love for Yeats, because it instils positivism in the readers and also because it showcases Smith's mastery of classical imagery, romantic form (ode) and Irish landscape.

3

Sharpness Cutting Sharpness: Smith's Imagist Poetry

Smith wrote in a letter to Desmond Pacey: "Metaphysical poetry and pure poetry are what I stood and stand for" (Pacey: *Ten Canadian Poets* 203). The poems which Smith published in the second sections of *Collected Poems* (1962) and *Poems, New and Collected* (1967) are broadly categorized as "imagistic" (Woodcock: "Turning New Leaves" 124). Most of these poems draw upon the theories and practices of the imagists in varying degrees and in different ways to present an external nature that is distinctly Canadian.

Smith was familiar with imagist poetry and poetics. He writes of imagism in the "Rejected Preface" to *New Provinces* (1936): "The imagist . . . seeks with perfect objectivity and impersonality to recreate a thing or arrest an experience as precisely and vividly and simply as possible" (8). He states in his "Introduction" to *The Book of Canadian Poetry* (1943): "The modern revival began in the twenties with a simplification of technique. . . . Canadian poets turned against rhetoric, sought a sharper, more objective imagery, and limited themselves as far as possible to the language of everyday and the rhythms of speech" (28). In an interview in 1974, he tells Heenan: "We were rather strong for imagism because of its conciseness" (Online).

Based on such knowledge of imagism, Smith's imagistic lyrics are brief, written in free verse, and partake of objectivity and impersonality which are considered the hallmarks of imagism. In other aspects, Smith made shades of change in conventional imagism. He made these changes in the light of the characteristic Canadian content, environment and ecology of his poetry. In addition, Smith's imagist poems concentrate on metaphysical perceptions. They are, as Anne Compton states, "intellectual probes" ("After the ebb-flow", 55). To comprehend these changes and concepts, it is essential to know the general principles and practices of imagism.

Conventional Imagism

Imagism was a movement in early twentieth century English poetry. It favoured precision of imagery and clear, sharp language. The imagists rejected the sentiment and moralizing tone of much of Victorian poetry. They also rejected their contemporaries, the Georgian poets, who were content to work within the Victorian tradition. Imagism called for directness of presentation and economy of language, as well as a willingness to experiment with non-traditional verse forms. Imagism is also significant historically as the first organized Modernist English language literary movement. Eliot remarks: "The *point de repère* usually and conveniently taken as the starting-point of modern poetry is the group denominated in London about 1910" (quoted in Brooker, 46).

The origins of imagism can be traced back to 1909 when Hulme and Flint met at the Eiffel Tower restaurant in London to discuss plans to reform contemporary poetry through free verse and the *tanka* and *haiku* and the removal of all unnecessary verbiage from poems. Hulme insisted on absolutely accurate presentation and no verbiage. Ezra Pound joined them later. The three were known as the "Eiffel Tower group."

Pound's studies of Arnaut Daniel, Dante, and Cavalcanti, led him to an admiration of the condensed, direct expression that he found in their writings. Pound writes of them: "You cannot get statement simpler than that, or clearer, or less rhetorical" (*Selected Prose,* 43). These criteria of directness, clarity and absence of rhetoric were to be the defining qualities of imagist poetry. In 1911, Pound introduced two other poets, Hilda Doolittle (H.D.) and her future husband Richard Aldington, to the Eiffel Tower group. These two were interested in exploring Greek poetic models, especially Sappho, an interest that Pound shared. The compression of expression that they achieved by following the Greek example complemented the imagist interest in Japanese poetry.

The new poetry of the imagist movement was welcomed immediately. In the United States, young poets such as Amy Lowell and William Carlos Williams, who had long chafed under the restrictions of traditional poetic forms, quickly took their cue from the imagists. The March 1913 issue of *Poetry* contained an essay entitled "Imagism" written by Pound. He defined an image as "that which presents an intellectual and emotional complex in an instant of time." He went on to state that "It is better to present one image in a lifetime than to produce voluminous works" ("A Retrospect", 374). The essay contained this significant statement of the group's position:

1. Direct treatment of the "thing," whether subjective or objective.
2. To use absolutely no word that does not contribute to the presentation.
3. As regarding rhythm: to compose in sequence of the musical phrase, not in sequence of the metronome.

In 1914, Pound collected an anthology of imagist verse under the title *Des Imagistes*. It was published by Harold Monro at the Poetry Bookshop in London, which was precisely the shop Smith visited during his brief sojourn in London during his adolescence in 1918-20. In all probability, Smith might have read this book. This anthology became one of the most important and influential collections of modernist verse. It included poems by Aldington, H.D., Amy Lowell, William Carlos Williams, James Joyce and Ford Madox Ford. The poems published offered a variety of types and influences, everything from *vers libre* to rhyming and prose poetry. The poems were short and bore the stamp of three main influences: classical Greek lyric, Japanese haiku, and recent French Symbolist poetry. Evidently, in a matter of a short time imagism had forced a sea-change in attitudes towards poetry in America and Britain.

But soon friction occurred between Pound and other members of the group. Hostility developed between Pound and Flint over their different interpretations of the history and goals of the group. Around this time, the American imagist Amy Lowell moved to London. The outcome was a series of imagist anthologies under the title *Some Imagist Poets*. The first of these appeared in 1915, planned and assembled mainly by H.D. and Aldington. Two further issues, both edited by Lowell, were published in 1916 and 1917. Lowell persuaded D. H. Lawrence to contribute poems to the volumes, making him the only writer to publish as both a Georgian poet and an imagist. Marianne Moore also became associated with the group during this period. Thus, when Lowell brought in such a diverse writer as D.H. Lawrence, the cohesion of the group quickly disappeared. Moreover, the times were hard for *avant-garde* literary movements with the World War I. The year 1917 marked the end of the imagism as a movement.

Despite the movement's short life, imagism had deeply influenced the course of modernist poetry in English. Aldington, in his 1941 memoir, writes: "I think the poems of Ezra Pound, H.D., Lawrence, and Ford Madox Ford will continue to be read. And to a considerable extent T. S. Eliot and his followers have carried on their operations from positions won by the imagists" (107).

A poet to find shortcomings in the imagist approach was Wallace Stevens. He remarks: "Not all objects are equal. The vice of imagism was that it did not recognize this" (quoted in Enck, 11). However, the influence of imagism can be seen clearly in the work of the Objectivist poets, who came to prominence in the 1930s under the guidance of Pound and Williams. The Objectivists worked mainly in free verse. Louis Zukofsky carried the imagist focus on formal concerns to a high level of development. Imagism influenced a number of poetry circles and movements in the 1950s, especially the Beat generation and the Black Mountain poets. Charles Olson, the theorist of the Black Mountain group, writes in his essay *Projective Verse*: "One perception must immediately and directly lead to a further perception" (17), his credo derived from and supplemented the imagists.

In practice, imagist poetry is written in crisp, descriptive, metaphorical language to achieve a clear expression without sentiment. An imagist poem has to focus on one object or concept; the object or concept has to be metaphorically described without referring to it explicitly; descriptions that sound emotional has to be avoided; it has to be in free verse with or without rhyme; it has to be direct, clear, and should not directly sympathize or romanticize the target object or concept. William Carlos Williams' "The Red Wheelbarrow" with its precise imagery and economy of words is the best example of an imagist poem.

From this brief analysis of the origin, development and legacy of the imagist poetry, it is understandable that cotemporary poets like Charles Olson and Louis Zukofsky have been using modified, personalized forms of imagism. Similarly, Smith has customized conventional imagist principles to suit his requirement.

Smith's Imagism

Smith is indebted to Hulme for his brand of philosophical imagism. Hulme considers the metaphysics of the imagist movement as derived from the philosopher Henri Bergson whose work he translated. Bergson believed that we grasp a thing only by "rational thinking" which he termed as "intuition." By intuition, he meant the "kind of intellectual sympathy by which one places oneself within an object in order to coincide with what is unique in it" (Bergson, 23-4). According to Bergson, the intuitive faculty ("intellectual sympathy") of the viewer receives the objects in an image and the image, in turn, communicates the thing discovered. Smith also sees an object with the "intellectual sympathy" which the imagists value, but in addition to that he also practises the "analysis" which they condemn.

Bentley has clearly emphasized this aspect of Smith's imagism by suitably designating his article on Smith's imagist poetry as "Not of Things only, but of Thought." The imagists valued only the "thing"; Smith valued the "thing" and also the "thought." Smith's imagist poems grasp not merely the fact, but the meaning of the fact. The seventeenth-century metaphysical poet Thomas Traherne writes: "Apprehensions within are better than their objects" (323). Similarly, Smith believes that the thought of an object is better than the object itself because it brings the object closer than mere representation.

Smith's imagism is based on the assumption that natural world is constituted of relations among things. Relation is thus built into the poems. His poems are single image or single scene poems: a creek, a cliff, a current, a stony strand or a flower. The objects are small and ordinary and the poet presents them in a concentrated and brief manner. Smith's focus is always the prospect or an object in the prospect where things edge into one another, a scene of confluence of interactive elements.

Smith's imagist poems have a structural similarity. In each poem there are two main stages linked by an interim third stage. The first stage is "seeing"; then there is a "turn"; and the turn is followed by "bonding." The interim "turn" stage is generally signalled by a pivotal word. The two-stage "seeing" and "bonding" captures the rapport among objects, and the rapport between object and viewer. The first stage, "seeing," fixes the image in time. It introduces the object. The second stage, "analysis," presents the object in relation to other objects and in relation to time. This is the narrative stage. Smith's focus is on the cumulative function of "seeing" and "analyzing." This is contrary to the practice of other imagists. Other imagists seek a singular effect; Smith aims at a collective effect. Smith makes an intuitive grasp of the object like the imagists; but, after that grasp, unlike the imagists, he includes a narrative movement.

Obviously the fundamental difference between Smith's imagist poetry and that of other imagists is that Smith presents objects in relation and in time; the imagists fix the image in time only. Smith's practice of imagism is closer to the theories of Ernest Fennollosa who observes: "Thought is successive . . . because the operations of nature are successive" (57). Smith distinguishes his range of imagism from conventional imagism thus: "The purpose of an imagist poem is to perceive and to present perceptions, but here we go further in an effort to grasp the idea of the thing and of its place in history" ("F.R. Scott and Some of His Poems", 35).

An examination of Smith's "imagistic" poems is now undertaken to show the complexity of his creative response to imagist ideas.

The Two Birds (1926)

"The Two Birds" was originally published as "Something Apart." The poem is in three stanzas of seven lines each. Smith uses emotional symbols to describe an austere ambience in the poem. Being Smith's earliest imagist poem, his unique imagist skills are not applied properly in the poem and are indistinct. The poet is in a landscape, here a pinewood; he is not aligned to it as in other imagist poems but is alienated from it by his own foulness. The first stanza reads:

So I went into the cool
Pinewoods where the yellow sun falls
Into a steel-gray pool
And heard at irregular intervals
The angular creaking note
That is forced rather than falls
From the cat-bird's ragged throat.

The word "So" which begins the poem is significant. It serves two purposes. Firstly, it gets the immediate attention of the reader to the situation. Secondly, it refers to some distressing event which has brought the poet to the pinewood. The woods to which the poet has resorted, as a result of some unspecified event, is a radiant world of "cool sweet air." Thc world is connected with heaven by "the gold sun's winding stair." In such a romantic environment, the poet is disturbed to hear the "creaking note" of the cat-bird:

Breaking the cool sweet air
Under the columns of pine
And the cold sun's winding stair.

Hours pass by. Scenes are changing. But the bird continues its shrill note. Identification is struck between the poet and the bird now. The erstwhile "creaking note" is now identified with the voice of the poet:

> I heard what the solitary cried
> In a voice as twisted as mine.

Meanwhile, the sun has set. Everything is still, crystal-like stillness everywhere. But, two things – the bird and the poet – do not contribute to this stillness. Identification struck in the second stanza, ends in affirmation in the final lines. The second bird, the poet's black heart, is identified with the raucous bird:

> The wind and the water stood still,
> And stiller than these,
> As though the whole world were crystal,
> Only the raucous bird was something apart,
> As alien from all these
> As that other foul bird, my black heart.

The things in the poem are in a flux; but the condition of the poet and the bird is static. They are in eternal despair. As Smith himself has said, the poem expresses "bitterness, remorse, and self-disgust." Smith connects the heart's condition in "The Two Birds" with the bitter king who fled the "fat royal life" in anger in "Proud Parable."

The Creek (1928)

"The Creek," "Swift Current" and "Sea Cliff" are companion poems. They discuss water and shore, firmness and flux. Recurrences of some words like "ragged" and "wisps" provide the connecting link. The two stages of "seeing" and "analysis" characteristic of Smith's imagist poems are marked-off by some technique in each of the poem.

"The Creek" presents a continuous interaction between water and shore focusing on a variety of objects – stones, roots, grass and herbs – at the stream's edge:

Stones
still wet with cold black earth,
roots, whips of roots
and wisps of straw,
green soaked crushed leaves
mudsoiled where hoof has touched them,
twisted grass
and hairs of herbs
that lip the ledge of the stream's edge:
these

Alliteration and consonance provide an exquisite rhythm and draw attention to the quality of each object. The use of "lip" as a verb in "lip the ledge," and the already "crushed leaves" becoming "mudsoiled" because of the stepping on it of the hoof evoke a subtle and delicate sensibility. The variety of objects "that lip the ledge of the stream's edge" recalls a similar observation by A.K. Ramanujam in his poem "A River." It reads:

A river dries to a trickle
in the sand,
baring the sand-ribs
straw and women's hair
clogging the watergates
at the rusty bars
under the bridges with patches
of repair all over them.

The imagery of the "sand-ribs / straw and women's hair / clogging the water gates" in "A River" is a typical repetition of "wisps of straw, / . . . twisted grass / and hairs of herb / that lip the ledge of the stream's edge" in "The Creek." This analogous viewing of two unrelated poets is characteristic of their archetypal perception.

In Smith's poem, the perception shifts from the creek to the water:

Then foamfroth, waterweed,
and windblown bits of straw

that rise, subside, float wide,
come round again, subside,
a little changed
and stranger, nearer
nothing:
these

A churning action takes place and the action is broken into discrete movements to show the enormity of flux, transformation and resurrection of the object. "Break the world all into parts," said Traherne, "examine them asunder" (176), and that is what Smith appears to be doing here. A resourceful reader will be reminded here of the purification of the soul in bits and pieces in *The Waste Land* in the section on "Death by Water":

A current under sea
Picked his bones in whispers. As he rose and fell
He passed the stages of his age and youth
Entering the whirlpool. (315-18)

The reference is to the fertility god of the pagan rituals whose image was thrown into the water as a symbol of fertility and resurrected again in the spring. Eliot suggests death by water as a source of salvation of our sins; thereupon we are absolved of our sins.

In Smiths' poem, the listing of things undergoing change – "waterweed" and "bits of straw" – parallels the listing in the first stanza. Since this is a stanza of movement and change, verbs dominate: "rise," "float," "subside" and "changed." Movement shows the things little changed but in actuality nothing is changed. What is seen is the continuous interaction between water and shore; what is understood is constancy and flux. The continuity of action is represented in this poem by the separation of the word "these" at the end of each stanza and not completing the action with a full-stop. In effect the word "these" leads to repetition of the action again and again infinitely.

The "nothing" of the poem finds a wider application in Smith's poems on death and in the scheme of his Neo-Platonic theories. The whole poem is a description of the process of "reductive metamorphosis" (Djwa: "Of Metaphysics and Dry Bones", 23). It may also be noticed that Smith is consistent with imagist theory and practice in constructing his poem out of "diverse images borrowed from very different orders of things" (Bergson, 11), in this instance, external landscape. Ferns rightly remarks that "The Creek" is a "delicate and subtle work of imagistic mimesis" (43).

Leon Edel, in his detailed analysis of "The Creek" in "The Worldly Muse of A.J.M. Smith" remarks that the very shape of the poem is human. He writes: "The very shape of the poem as we hold it up to the light is human; there are two bodies in the two stanzas, and the bodies are male and female. The first stanza is all female and the second is male" (207). Not only do its two stanzas represent respectively the female and male profiles, but the "effects of craft" – assonance, internal rhymes, mimetic rhythms, and the rest – contrive to render the apparently literal vocal of anthropomorphic significance. It should be noticed that in the first (female) section of the poem, the terms that are open to humanistic interpretation ("wet", "whips," "wisps," "hair," "lip") are, so to say, buried within lines of naturalistic description and that in the second (male) section figure and ground become one in the rhythms of natural and human life.

Bentley states: "Smith's 'Creek' is no sweet river that runs softly in song. It is, however, humanizing and liberating, an ecologically appropriate and mischievously provocative adaptation of an imported aesthetic to the demands of its Canadian environment" ("Not of Things Only, But of Thought", 33).

Smith himself describes "The Creek" as an example of the "simpler kind of imagist verse," though he adds, as if to stress the importance of style in the poem: "the reader may notice that the development of the poem depends upon metrical devices as much as on images; the music is harsh and the rhythm difficult" ("A Rejected Preface", 8). It is wise to conclude, like Anne Compton, that in "The Creek," "in an objective response which is both sensual and intellectual, Smith discovers form in nature" (62).

Swift Current (1930)

"Swift Current" is a remarkably analytical poem which defines itself through metaphor, negation and abstraction. It proceeds by description, negation and comparison. The wind is described in the first two lines:

> This is a visible
> and crystal wind:

Then, the stillness of water is presented in negatives:

> no ragged edge,
> no splash of foam,
> no whirlpool's scar;

But the stillness is in fact swiftness, which is noticeable "only / -in the narrows" where the course of water is constricted by the limits of space. The rapidity of the current makes the things invisible to the poet; hence he uses a sequence of metaphors to describe its swiftness:

> only
> –in the narrows,
> sharpness cutting sharpness,
> arrows of direction,
> spears of speed.

The words "edge" and "scar" in the initial lines anticipate the military metaphors in the later lines. The swift current is compared to a clash of blades – "sharpness cutting sharpness"— an arrow and a spear. The concurrence of natural images with martial images insists upon the sharpness of the current than its swiftness. The perception here is opposite to that of "The Creek" where the poet has an illusion of some change taking place when nothing actually changes.

In this poem, a change is taking place but there is an illusion of nothing happening ("no ragged edge, / no splash of foam, / no whirlpool's scar"). In other words, it does not emphasize the visual content which is so indispensable to the imagists. Ferns states that "it is much easier to visualize Smith's creek than his swift current" (43). Bentley attributes this non-visual quality of the poem to the Canadian landscape. He writes: "[The poem] focuses on a feature of the [Canadian] landscape which, though 'visible', lacks the texture, sounds, shapes and anthropomorphic possibilities" ("Not of Things Only, But of Thought", 35). This may also be the reason A.M. Klein calling the poem "strictly Canadian" (258).

The imagistic focus on the "thing" as "thing" also mirrors contemporary developments in modern art, especially cubism. Although imagism isolates objects through the use of what Ezra Pound called "luminous details," Pound's Ideogram Method of juxtaposing concrete instances to express an abstraction is similar to cubism's manner of synthesizing multiple perspectives into a single image (Michael Davidson, 11-3), because "an isolated thing does not exist in nature" (Fennolosa, 60).

Similarly Bentley interprets "Swift Current" from the point-of-view of cubism. The effect of the final lines of the poem ("arrows of direction, / spears of speed"), according to Bentley, is to allow the reader alternately to view either the vectored signs – "arrows" and "spears" – or the swift current. While the poem's title, "Swift Current," should ensure that, finally, the water rather than the vectors will be in the foreground in the reader's mind, the abstract, yet visual, quality of "arrows of direction / spears of speed" also ensures that, when attention is paid to these as one-dimensional, representational signs which are, nevertheless, inseparable from the water, the reader gains an impression as of a cubist painting.

Finally, the attentive reader would leave the poem, aware that a difficult, and almost scientific, process of observation, analysis, and description has happened in the poem. The reader would also be aware that under the pressure of a rational and imaginative engagement with his intractable subject-matter, Smith brilliantly, and in an almost painterly manner, has succeeded in rendering the swift current dynamically visible and altogether intelligible.

Sea Cliff (1930)

"Sea Cliff" gives the impression of having been written from "inside the object." It presents a picture of the ebb and flow of the waves on a rock. The poem is in two stages of nine lines each. The first section describes the wave; the second section describes the falling of the waves on the rock. The lineation of the poem represents the ebb and flow of the waves. In the first three lines, two lines of paired nouns, joined by the same preposition, are followed by a rest line:

> Wave on wave
> and green on rock
> and white between

This pattern is repeated, but whereas the first three lines present movement and sight, the next three lines describe movement and sound:

> the splash and black
> the crash and hiss
> of the feathery fall

The remaining three lines show the force of the waves:

> the snap and shock
> of the water wall
> and the wall of rock:

The lines in this poem and the other imagist poems are not capitalized to show that the occurrence is continuous. The verse is without a verb to demonstrate that the concentration is on the object and not on its action.

The poem, now, moves to the second stage: perception changes from the waves to the waves falling on the rock. The word "after" brings about the change; the word is repeated.

> after -
> after the ebb flow,
> wet rock,
> high-

high over the slapping green,
water sliding away
and the rock abiding,
new rock riding
out of the spray.

The first "after" marks a shift; the second belongs to the narrative. Now the attention is on action, and the continuity of action, which is marked-off by the present-participles "slapping," "sliding," "abiding" and "riding." There is magnified and concentrated attention on each wave falling on the rock and then subsiding. During each ebb-tide a new rock appears, during each flood-tide the old rock disappears. The rock is what it was and also new. There is a similitude of change, but no change is taking place.

"Sea Cliff," like "Swift Current" and "The Creek," has caused stereotyped critical opinion in sexual terms. Leon Edel has shown that the poems are structured on an "underground of sex" ("The Worldly Muse of A.J.M. Smith", 208). He has shown that in "Swift Current" phallic arrows and spears opposed to the "whirlpool's scar," and in "Sea Cliff," wave surrounding rock, while the rock thrusts up through the water, "new rock riding / out of the spray" are instances of sexual connotation.

Bentley identifies the presence of a sexual rhythm and human resonances in the poem. He writes that the poem "suggests both a sexual rhythm and an enduring strength which have clear, human referents. . . . A full response to 'Sea Cliff' will recognize that, true to its imagist origins, the poem is more than a recreation of the kinesis and stasis of things; it is an invitation to discover the human significance of the sea's rhythm and the rock's endurance" ("Not of Things Only, But of Thought", 31).

But humanization of nature is against the normal imagist practice. It is specifically this humanization of nature that Smith objects to in his "Rejected Preface." Anne Compton is also against finding a sexual rhythm or enduring human values in Smith's poems on nature. She writes: "For Smith, nature does not mirror the human. The only connection between the two is that which occurs when the senses are open and the intellect comprehends. This brings nature closer than any imparting to it of human values, sexual or spiritual" ("After the ebb-flow", 60).

John Ferns looks at "Sea Cliff" merely as an "imagistic piece of verbal representation of the movement of the sea" (42). He calls attention to some of the stylistic devices, which include alliteration, repetition, consonance, assonance, end-rhyme, and rhythmical variation that Smith musters to enact the contours and movements of his seascape.

Gordon Harvey disputes that in "'Sea Cliff' style is more noticeable than subject" (8). What Harvey fails to see is that for a Canadian poet rhetoric and style are a means of asserting individual and social values in the context of a landscape that is devoid of human resonances. Hence, "Sea Cliff" should be considered as an example of Smith's affirmation of "the triumph of beauty or love or strength or of spiritual values generally over all those forces, natural and social, which seek to overwhelm them" (Pacey: *Ten Canadian Poets,* 215).

The Lonely Land (1926)

"The Lonely Land" is the most-anthologized, most revised and much discussed poem of Smith. It first appeared as "The Lonely Land: Group of Seven" in *McGill Fortnightly Review* in January 1926. It was revised and published in *Canadian Forum* in July 1927. It appeared in *The New Outlook* in October 1927 after another revision. The fourth version of the poem appeared in *The Dial* in June 1929. When it appeared in *News of the Phoenix* in 1943, the title was shortened to "The Lonely Land." After a study of various probable influences in composing the poem, three sources are short-listed: Yeatsian romanticism, H. D's imagism and Group of Seven paintings of Canada.

Smith presents in the poem a landscape filled with both beauty and conflict. He uses imagery and language effectively to establish that beauty can be derived from conflict. The poem begins in an atmosphere of conflict. He presents a "grey and cloud-piled sky," and fills the favourable image with cedar and "jagged fir," a ruthless and harsh image. He then goes on to describe a bay with spume at its edges:

Cedar and jagged fir
uplift sharp barbs
against the gray
and cloud-piled sky;
and in the bay
blown spume and windrift
and thin, bitter spray
snap
at the whirling sky;
and the pine
trees lean one way.

A ceaseless wind bending the cedar, fir and pine trees, and spume blowing high in the air, the scenery is characteristic of rough and rugged North Canadian landscape. But the concept of water ("bay") is most often associated with a sense of calm. So, the poem is an appreciation of discordant beauty.

Linguistic use of participles instead of straight verbs – "jagged fir," "cloud-piled sky," "blown spume" – is an effective imagistic technique Smith learned from Ross, which, for example, Ross popularized in his poem "By the Shore":

Down by the
shore hangs a
branch of the pale-stemmed
trembling leafed poplar.

The participles in the expression "pale-stemmed / trembling leafed poplar" are unusual. Both Ross and Smith employ participles as verb-alternatives with great effect.

The verbs "uplift," "snap" and "lean" in the foregoing stanza suggest strong and forceful action. These forceful visual images are interwoven with the emotional and enthusiastic call of the duck in the second stanza:

A wild duck calls
to her mate,
and the ragged
and passionate tones
stagger and fall,

and recover,
and stagger and fall,
on these stones -
are lost
in the lapping of water
on smooth, flat stones.

The duck calls out to her mate, but her calls go unnoticed as they are lost on the stone by the water's edge. The images arouse a sense of loneliness. In addition to the visual conflict already present, the poet now feels an emotional conflict. However, while the poet is at odds, he brings in a sense of hope and optimism. He uses the words "lapping" and "smooth" at the end of the stanza to quieten his inner turmoil and prepare himself for the change of mood in the next stanza. He recognizes that perhaps there is a beauty to be seen and heard in the way the wind causes to pines to bend, in the way it "curdles the sky," in the way the landscape, in spite of the conflict, has survived.

In the third stanza, the poet resolves the conflict using the words "dissonance" and "resonance" thereby softening the image and presenting a sense of change and optimism. Obviously, the violent and broken images abstracted from the ragged landscape are the "beauty of dissonance":

This is a beauty
of dissonance,
this resonance
of stony strand,
this smoky cry
curled over a black pine
like a broken
and wind-battered branch
when the wind
bends the tops of the pines
and curdles the sky
from the north.

The poet and the reader achieve intense, though austere, delight in this unsympathetic landscape. After a heartfelt perception of this discordant beauty the poem ends in a coda (a coda is an independent passage introduced after the natural conclusion of a poem):

> This is the beauty
> of strength
> broken by strength
> and still strong.

"The Lonely Land" has an interesting publication history. When Smith first published the poem in 1926, the theme was the descri-ption of nature, the landscape was Northern Canada and the style was Yeatsian romanticism. In Canada, in the 1920s, around the time the poem was written, a spirit of individualism and nationalism prevailed in art and literature. The "Group of Seven" was formed with the aim of propagating nationalism through landscape painting and by conduct of exhibitions. For the idea of "The Lonely Land," Smith was influenced by the Group of Seven in three aspects: the title, the description of the landscape, and the theme of conflict in elements. First, the title combines the captions of two paintings by MacDonald, "The Lonely North" and "The Solemn Land." Second, the landscape is a collage of many paintings and comments of the Group of Seven painters. Third, the details Smith selected for inclusion in "The Lonely Land" emphasize, on the one hand, those aspects of the landscape that are inhospitable or actively threatening to life (the "snap" of the "bitter spray" implies an active hostility) and, on the other hand, those features of the landscape ("Cedar," "fir," and "pine trees," the "wild duck" and "her mate") whose very existence is an affirmation of life. This conflict of the elements and the last lines of the poem, the coda, are adaptations of Varley's canvas, "Stormy Weather Near Georgian Bay," which expresses "the rhythmic movement of swirling water against solid rock and bending pines" (Djwa: "A New Soil and a Sharp Sun", 12).

The poem illustrates Smith's care in textual revision. Pacey truly mentions that these changes make the poem tighter, "More concrete and exact" (*Ten Canadian Poets,* 214). "The Lonely Land" and "The Two Birds" appeared in *The McGill Fortnightly* in the same year. Smith has mentioned that a "brief bit" was taken over from "Something Apart," the first version of "The Two Birds," and worked into "The Lonely Land" ("A Self-Review," *Towards a View,* 212). The original poems were similar enough to allow a transfer of phrases. The poet seeks relief in the landscape in both the poems. In "Something Apart," Smith seeks reprieve from "the sorrow in my heart"; in "The Lonely Land," he wants to "Find for a tired heart relief" in the landscape. However, in "The Two Birds," the poet, like the bird, is something apart, alienated from everything in the pinewoods. In "The Lonely Land," the poet hopes to find solace in the landscape.

A comparison of a stanza from the first version of "The Lonely Land" and the corresponding stanza from the latest version of the poem will throw light on many more things. The first version as published in *The McGill Fortnightly* in 1926 reads:

> It is good to come to this land
> Of desolate splendour and grey grief,
> And on a lone, stony strand
> Find for a tired heart relief
> In a wild duck's bitter cry –

The corresponding stanza in the latest version when it appeared in *News of the Phoenix* in 1943 reads:

> A wild duck calls
> to her mate,
> and the ragged
> and passionate tones
> stagger and fall,
> and recover,
> and stagger and fall.

Between the two versions, depersonalization has taken place at two levels. Firstly, Smith has attempted to hold back personal feelings by removing the line "Find for a tired heart relief" from the first version. Secondly, he has tried to be objective by giving sharp, concentrated attention to the duck's bitter cry: "stagger and fall / and recover, / and stagger and fall."

Secondly, Smith has caused a change of technique from Yeatsian romanticism to H.D.'s imagism. The images in the first stanza, those of cedar and fir uplifting "sharp barbs," as well as the rhythmic movement of spume and windrift, are clearly derived from H.D.'s "Oread":

> Whirl up, sea -
> whirl your pointed pines,
> splash your great pines
> On our rocks,
> hurl your green over us,
> Cover us with your pools of fir.

But Smith's poem is much more imagistic than H. D.'s short lyric. It is catalogic in nature, listing significant details in an accumulative manner which is appropriate to Canada's open and stretching landscape. By a difficult poetic experiment, Smith has adapted the imagist mode to the needs of an imaginative vision and understanding of the Canadian North. "The Lonely Land" remains one of the best poems of Canadian poetry. It is indeed a "Canadian classic" (Pacey: *Ten Canadian Poets,* 212).

Walking in a Field, Looking Down and Seeing a White Violet (1963)

In this poem Smith makes a configuration very different from others poems, one which is organic than scientific, making this poem more intimate and less abstract, more romantic and less objective. Smith very clearly presents the subjective, romantic view of nature in this poem. As the very title "Walking in a Field, Looking Down and Seeing a White Violet" suggests, this is a poem concerned with ways of "seeing." The eyes survey the field in the first stanza:

> Threading
> the ragged edges
> of meadowgrass
> and avid arches
> of tendril
> and torn leaves

and straws
of last year's grass
and strings
of crass cornwisps
windwafted
from last year's
sheaves

The eye is engaged in the activity of "Threading" its way among the objects, shapes, and textures of a field in spring, making virtually no effort to do other than record the external nature through which it passes. The use of the coordinating conjunction "and" four times in this stanza insists on the process of "threading" that is going on in the mind of the poet.

The two stanzas correspond to the two-stage-seeing, "seeing" and "looking," and are linked by the phrase "the eye":

the eye
plays Jackstraws
to disentangle
the sykwhite skyblue
first shy white shoot
of a white violet
lifting a graygreen stalk
out of the welter
of leafgreen grassgreen
folded over the old
grayblack earth's
mothermilky
breast

In the arrangement of the stanzas, "the eye" is centrally located. The eye is passive in the first stanza. It becomes active in the second stanza where the eye is more consciously directed; it "plays Jackstraws / to disentangle / the skywhite skyblue / first shy white shoot / of a white violet." In the use of compound adjectives in the poem, there is an underlying assumption that small particulars of nature can yield lofty meanings to the visionary eye.

The eye distinguishes between "skywhite" and "skyblue"; between "graygreen" and "grayblack"; and between "leafgreen" and "grassgreen." The colour symbolism is religious – white for purity, blue which is Mary's colour, and green the colour of life and growth – but the subject-matter is secular. As suggested by Djwa ("Of Metaphysics and Dry Bones", 25), behind the conclusion "earth's / mothermilky / breast" is the discovery of physical and spiritual regeneration symbolized by the flower the "mother-root" of George Herbert's poem "The Flower":

> . . . as flowers depart
> To see their mother-root, when they have blown,
> Where they together
> All the hard weather,
> Dead to the world, keep house unknown. (10-4)

Wild Raspberry (1958)

Smith dedicated "Wild Raspberry" to W.W.E. Ross. In this poem written three decades after the Creek series there is a clear change of perception. In the Creek series perception led to abstraction; here perception leads to pleasure. This is one of Smith's typical romantic poems. The poem is directly addressed to the raspberry making it more personal. The poem is in seven couplets. The first six couplets relate to the seeing; the last couplet relates to the analysis. In the first two couplets Smith presents the raspberry plant before the rain:

> Your ragged leaves
> are speckled with dust
>
> They are frayed at the edges
> and sticky with sunshine

The leaves of the plant are ragged, frayed, dusty and sticky because of heat and sunshine. In the next four couplets, Smith describes the plant after the rain:

> but after the rain
> gashes of red

glisten
among slippery green leaves

Yellow whips
and prickly little branches

are pulled into curves
by the big berries.

The rain has given a new lease of life to the sun-burnt raspberry leaves. The rain has changed the "ragged leaves" to "slippery green." The vision is pleasant and colourful with splashes of red, green and yellow. The eye feasts and feels refreshed because of these sensual delights. The poem ends in a declaration of contentment:

The eye feasts on them
And feels refreshed

As an imagist activity, the poem shows the kinship between imagist simultaneity and metaphysical wit, but this final couplet acquires the force of a critique of the imagist emphasis of sight and the sensual over thought and the metaphysical.

W.W.E. Ross, to whom the poem is dedicated, suggested replacing "feels" in the last line with "is" (Michael Darling: "The letters of W.W.E. Ross to Smith", 110). Smith did not carry out the suggestion because he felt the subjective, content verb "feels" would be more emphatic than the objective, structure verb "is." Obviously, Smith wanted to give importance to the sensual.

In such a context, "Wild Raspberry" can be seen as an antithesis to "The Two Birds." All the sensuous images evoked in this poem were present in the old poem too. But Smith, then, did not have the mind to see and appreciate such things. It has taken thirty years for him to find communion with nature.

Stylistically, although "Wild Raspberry" is dedicated to W.W.E. Ross, the poem's lines are arranged in couplets, a form not at all typical of Ross, but, rather, suggestive of William

Carlos Williams's work in the imagist or objectivist mode. Bentley has made an analysis of Williams's influence on Smith in composing the poem and has suggested that such couplet poems as Williams' "Nantucket" and "Flowers by the Sea" might have been the referents for "Wild Raspberry." The poem is less subtle in remembering Williams's famous "Red Wheelbarrow," whose lines are also arranged in groups of two, making what in essence is a verbal and visual allusion from its own "after the rain / gashes of red / glisten / among slipp'ry green leaves" to the "red wheel / barrow / glazed with rain / water / beside the white/chickens" of Williams' poem.

The Convolvulus (1958)

The last poem to be considered here and the final poem of Smith's imagist group is "The Convolvulus." It was published as a companion poem to "Wild Raspberry." The (romantic) pleasure which Smith gathered in "Wild Raspberry" is confirmed in "The Convolvulus." While its fundamental technique derives from imagism, the poem is a dynamic statement of a joyful celebration of life and living. The title is appropriate. The convolvulus flower convolves, or encloses, all the "raggedness" of Smith's previous imagist poems – "ragged edge" ("Swift Current"), "ragged / and passionate tones" ("The Lonely Land"), "ragged edges of meadowgrass" ("Walking in a Field") and "ragged leaves" ("Wild Raspberry").

The convolvulus flower closes at night and opens in the morning. When reared in a home-garden the flower is called morning-glory; when it grows by itself in hedge and ditch it is called bindweed. Though it looks pleasant, it is tough and vigorous.

The poem is in the nature of an ode addressed to the flower calling upon it to unfold its petals to affirm life:

> Open your narrow throat,
> convolvulus, and cry
>
> let your paean of being
> ring like a great shout

distinguished
in the diapason

of the yellow sun
and million green shoots

in the communion of summer
and the morning's glory

The blossoming of the flower is likened to the singing of an anthem of life ("paean of being") in a grand-chorus ("in the diapason") of the "yellow sun /and million green shoots." The poet universalizes the new-found pleasure the poet is enjoying. The conflict formed in "The Two Birds" has at last found its harmony in "The Convolvulus." In "The Two Birds" Smith generalized his sorrow by sharing it with another bird. In "The Convolvulus" he universalizes his happiness ("communion of summer") by sharing it with nature.

"The Convolvulus" is a good poem on which to conclude because it points up some of the enduring qualities of Smith's imagistic poems: their celebrating energy, their rhetorical skill, their linguistic brilliance, their memorable cadences, and, above all, their combination of vividness and intelligence. Smith's tendency to describe as well as to analyze may push some of his imagistic poems farther into the realm of the abstract than some readers may wish to accept. But that intellection and abstraction may well be a necessary and correct response to the Canadian ecosystem and environment.

To sum up, few Canadian poets have written of nature as objectively as Smith. Smith adopts the imagist practice of seeing the thing in itself, but he subjects what he sees to analysis. Where he differs from the imagists, he resembles Thomas Traherne, whose notion of imagism includes analysis and appreciation. "If nature is infused with glory, analysis discovers, not destroys it," writes Anne Compton (72). The study of Smith's imagist poems is a process of progression from agony to ecstasy. The agony of "The Two Birds" leads to the abstractions of the Creek-series poems; an understanding and appreciation is formulated in "The Lonely Land" and confirmed in "Wild Raspberry"; this understanding universalized in "The Convolvulus."

4

A Bandolier Full of Kodak Films: Smith's Social Satires

Most of Smith's social satires were written during the decade between 1930 and 1940. This was an interim period in his career between the imagist poems and the poems on death. He describes in these poems the falsities and the dissipation of the illusionist modern society, which he likened to "a bandolier full of Kodak films." Michael Darling rightly calls these poems "socio-metaphysical" ("A.J.M. Smith" 255).

The change of genre is partly because of change of sojourn from Canada to America where he had found a job and shifted in 1936. And it is also because of the dreadful contemporary social conditions – economic depression, unemployment, fascism and the fears of war. But the immediate and more valid reason for the change is an article by Leo Kennedy. In the article entitled "Directions for Canadian Poets" published in 1936, Leo Kennedy had criticized Smith for his failure to concern himself with socially conscious verse or "social reality" (22). This remark and other such adverse remarks forced Smith to publish a bunch of social satires.

Many of Smith's satires appeared only around1936 when Kennedy's article was published. "Son and Heir" appeared in 1935, "Noctambule" in 1936, "Far West" in 1939 and "Ode: The Eumenides" appeared in 1942. These poems had the desired impact. They enhanced Smith's reputation among the critics. In 1944, while reviewing *News of the Phoenix* in the *Manitoba Arts Review,* E.K. Brown wrote that Smith's theory of poetry "leaves an honoured place for satire and light verse" ("A.J.M.

Smith and the Poetry of Pride" 31). He added that Smith's "disgust with bourgeois values has a searing strength" (32). He even said that Smith's satires should be read first as preparation for the more difficult and important pieces.

Smith's satires are not didactic. His aim in his social poems is not amelioration of society. They do not focus on specific events, nor do they criticize individuals or institutions. These poems are merely personal observations of Smith of the impact of the modern world on other individuals. He does not have comforting words for the victims of society whose plight he describes in his poems. George Woodcock writes: "As a satirist he [Smith] believed that the poet had the right to mock the world, but he did not believe he had the ability to change it, and so his satire was mainly directed to manners" (*Canadian Writers and their Works,* 13). It is because of this lack of social commitment Smith was not considered a popular satirist. But his poems are the best as records of societal observation.

Smith uses surrealistic images abundantly in his satires. His love of paradox helps him to capture the ironies of the modern world. He describes a society that prefers the comfort of illusion to the real, a generation which prefers the meretricious present to the genuine past.

News of the Phoenix (1933)

In "News of the Phoenix," Smith mocks gently at the tendency of modern bureaucracies to suppress unfavourable news. He wrote the poem in the cliché-ridden jargon of the bureaucrats:

> They say the Phoenix is dying, some say dead.
> Dead without issue is what one message said,
> But that has been suppressed, officially denied.
>
> I think myself the man who sent it lied.
> In any case, I'm told, he has been shot,
> As a precautionary measure, whether he did or not.

The poem is in the manner of Auden's satires. The phrase "officially denied" is a euphemism of authority expressing suppression of fact. "As a precautionary measure" is a truism used in the bureaucracy. Smith uses these terms very effectively and sarcastically in this poem.

The messenger is blamed for the message and "has been shot." The irony of the situation is that the officials who are responsible for the shooting of the messenger either do not understand the true nature of the Phoenix or they do not bother to know the facts. Phoenix is a mythical bird which, after living hundreds of years in the Arabian desert, burnt itself on a funeral pyre and rose from the ashes young again to live another cycle of life. The Phoenix can never be extinct, or be "dead without issue." The message must have been in error and the messenger shot for no reason. Smith mocks at the foolishness of the officials.

Smith employs double irony in the poem as the narrator of the poem himself is not sure of the message: "I think myself the man who sent it lied." The poem is a superb ironical revelation of one's inability to distinguish between true and false where propaganda has replaced myth and the myth itself is considered a lie rather than a myth.

Son and Heir: 1930 (1935)

After lampooning the totalitarian society in "Phoenix," Smith now turns to domestic criticism in "Son and Heir: 1930." This poem ridicules a flunkey father and his son who is a victim of pampered affection and uncritical adulation. The poem is in movie-world slang. The first-stanza describes the birth of an heir to an affluent bourgeoisie:

> The nine-months-long-awaited heir is born,
> And the parents are pretty proud of the thing.
> Instinct censors any real, as too forlorn,
> Preview of coming attractions.

The description of the new-born as the "thing" in the second line gives the impression that the object of Smith's satire is the new-born. The pun on the word "real" (and "reel") is suggestive of the father's fascination for the tinsel world. He lives in an illusionary world of movies. He thinks of anything "real" as "forlorn" (illusory), anything forlorn as real ("Preview of coming attractions"). Having thus established the fake-reality of the father, Smith describes his illusions of the son in the next four stanzas in surrealistic images associated with the celluloid world:

> . . . Angels sing
>
> Like press agents the praises of their lamb
> In minds as polite as a mezzanine floor.
> They do concoct a brave, politic sham
> To ravel the plot, feature the smirking star.

The phrases, "press agents," "concoct," "sham," and "ravel the plot" anticipate and emphasize the fictional nature of the dream the parents have of the son. The following stanzas describe the dream:

> They see him innocency's Jaeger pelt
> Hide in the wolf's coat of angry youth,
> Striding over the very veldtlike veldt
> In a bandolier full of Kodak films.

The parents endow the boy a future with the attributes of a film-star Christ striding over the veldt (forest). Yet there is irony and self-mockery in this provenance as the reference to the Spanish bandolier implies. A more likely suggestion is that the bandolier will be filled not with bullets but with Kodak films and the veldt (forest) replaced by the barren landscape of the Spanish civil war. The dream continues:

> They make him up in the attractive role
> Of a he-god in the next episode,
> Bringing his woman dividends to roll
> A cigarette with, giving his old dad
>
> Market tips, and cigars on Father's Day,
> And his Mother telegrams and roses,
> Walking in rightwiseness, always au fait,
> Always sure of the thing he supposes.

The quality of the dream is cheap, but Smith emphasizes not only the cheapness, but also the danger of having dreams. The cosy-looking illusions projected by the parents are incongruous, resulting in double, sometimes, multiple illusions.

At this instance, the parents' dream is unexpectedly interrupted by a new and angry voice. The diction becomes ordinary replacing the illusionist, celluloid language:

> Who will turn the lights up on this show?
> You will find something has gone wrong with the switch,
> Or their eyes, used to horse opera, cannot grow
> Used to an ordinary son-of-a-bitch

This interruption is striking. It shocks the dreaming parents (and the readers) out of their complacency. Scene shifts from illusion to reality. The parents' plausibility which had almost toppled over into absurdity is brought under the tight control of fine parody. The "horse opera" of the parents end and the boy is presented as an ordinary naughty nitwit. The line, "Who will turn the lights up on this show?" recalls the opening line of another of Smith's poem, "Prothalamium": "Here in this narrow room there is no light." The line is also an example of Smith's use of such interrupting devices in his poems to break the narrative which later became an important postmodern stylistic device.

Now, as the shock of this interruption subsides, Smith charts out the dents that the post-war depression has made on contemporary society:

> Like you or me for a son, or the doom
> We discern – the empty years, the hand to mouth,
> The moving cog, the unattended loom,
> The breathless street, and lolling summer's drouth.

Smith closes the poem advising the illusion-clad parents and the readers to quit day-dreaming and face the realities:

> Let us keep melodrama out of this scene,
> Eye open to daylight, foot on the firm earth.

Smith's question "Who will turn the lights up on this show?" finds an answer in the concluding line "Eye open to daylight."

The question and the answer are powered by the imagery of light. The false and the simulated theatrical illumination prior to the question are contrasted with real and natural daylight in the answer.

The target of attack in "Son and Heir: 1930" is neither the boy, nor his parents, but the society. It is the society that has placed the parents on a pedestal and makes them see their son not as an ordinary man. But Smith has no comforting words for the boy as well. Smith, as is his wont, has played the role of a passive commentator and not an active reformer in this poem.

In "Noctambule" and "Far West" Smith is at his most complex mood, demanding the readers' ability to identify and appreciate a wide range of allusions that cause an apparently surreal vision. These poems, apart from being vigorous social satires, give credence to the view of Smith as a "socio-metaphysical" poet because Smith juxtaposes unrelated images, blends abstract ideas and human emotions in these poems.

Noctambule (1936)

"Noctambule," as the title suggests, is a kind of somnambular poem in which innocence is defeated by deception and traditional roles are reversed. Smith presents a series of surreal images in the first stanza:

> Under the flag of this pneumatic moon,
> - Blown up to bursting, whitewashed white,
> And painted like the moon - the piracies of day
> Scuttle the crank hulk of witless night.
> The great black innocent Othello of a thing
> Is undone by the nice clean pockethandkerchief
> Of 6 a.m., and though the moon is only an old
> Wetwash snotrag - horsemeat for good *rosbif* –

The real moon is replaced by an imitation – an over-blown pneumatic moon. Innocent night ("witless night") is betrayed by treacherous day ("piracies of day"). Night is described as "black innocent Othello" and day as "nice clean pockethandkerchief of 6 a.m.," the reference is to Iago.

At this stage of substitution, the poet undercuts and says that the society has taught people only to respect substitutions and worship the illusionary:

> Perhaps to utilize substitutes is what
> The age has to teach us.

However, here, in his usual self-contradictory manner, Smith exposes the fake quality of the new reality by the ubiquitous use of the word "utilize." He seems to imply that the substitution is only temporary and it is likely to be replaced by the real, if not, by another substitute, in course of time. Meanwhile, this acceptance of the substitution is dramatically intercepted by a fit of shell-shock ("the loud / Unmeaning warcry"):

> Wherefore let the loud
> Unmeaning warcry of treacherous daytime
> Issue like whispers of love in the moonlight,
> - Poxy old cheat!

In spite of the shellshock, the process of substitution continues until another shell-shock twitches the skin:

> So mewed the lion,
> Until mouse roared once and after lashed
> His tail: Shellshock came on again, his skin
> Twitched in the rancid margarine, his eye
> Like a lake isle in a florist's window:

A lion mews, a mouse roars and the shell shock occurs again. The skin shivers and the eyes glaze and withdraw. The glaze imagery has reference to Yeats's composition of "The Lake Isle of Innisfree." Yeats wrote the poem after gazing earnestly at a display in a florist's shop. His poem is thus a reflection of nature through the artefact, a make-believe substitution.

The last lines of Smith's poem are decisively satirical:

> Reality at two removes, and mouse and moon
> Successful.

The poem is a satire on the contemporary society. A series of surreal images in the first stanza lead to the direct comment, "Perhaps to utilize substitutes is what / The age has to teach us." The images in the last stanza lead to the sardonic observation, "Reality at two removes, and mouse and moon / Successful." We might think that the poem is a commentary against romanticism suggesting that "reality" is now to be associated with "substitutions" and "success." Looking a little more closely, we find that the poem progresses through a series of substitutions – paper moon for the real moon, treacherous day for innocent night, mouse for lion, florist's display for nature, and shell-shock for normalcy. All the images substituted are conditioned by the primary substitution, that of false moon for real, and the subsequent loss of beauty, innocence, strength, nature and poetry that were once associated with night and moon. In Smith's metaphor, night is an Othello, day an Iago. Having taken the modernist stand of accepting the substitute, Smith promptly has a fit of shell-shock. The poem, then, which might at first appear to be a repetition of the romantic or metaphysical vision traditionally associated with the term "Noctumble," is actually governed by nostalgia for those older values, now lost to an ersatz world. The thematic contrast is that of an "unmeaning" present to a more meaningful past.

Far West (1939)

"Far West" describes a young girl's sexual awakening at a cowboy movie. The girl, placed in a popcorn paradise (again, in a world of proxies), substitutes for poetry, love and God the sexual thrill of the movies:

> Among the cigarettes and the peppermint creams
> Came the flowers of fingers, luxurious and bland,
> Incredibly blossoming in the little breast.
>
> And in the Far West
> The tremendous cowboys in goatskin pants
> Shot up the town of her ignorant wish.

The word "ignorant" in the phrase "ignorant wish" strongly suggests that the girl is not a habitual sex-seeker, but is just about to become a victim of the ills of society. Again, like "Son and Heir," the satire is not on the girl but on the society. In this stanza, Smith makes use of different sound patterns to reinforce the contrasting sensory influences on the girl's consciousness. The plosives in the words "cigarettes," "peppermint," "bland" and "goatskin pants" represent a set of images, forceful and energetic like the "tremendous" cowboys. The fricatives in "flower of fingers" and "luxurious" represent another set of images which is insinuating and devious.

As the girl is watching the movies her thoughts wander. She remembers her reading of Tennyson which presents a contrasting situation:

> In the gun flash she saw the long light shake
> Across the lake, repeating that poem
> At Finsbury Park.

These lines allude to Tennyson's "The Splendour Falls on Castle Walls" in *The Princess*. The girl remembers reading "The long light shakes across the lakes." The next lines are also a reference to Tennyson:

> But the echo was drowned in the roll of the trams –
> Anyway, who would have heard?
> Not a soul! Not one noble and toxic like Buffalo Bill.

The first line recalls Tennyson's "Our echoes roll from soul to soul." Smith undercuts here to question ("Anyway, who would have heard?") how one could expect such people to know Tennyson and his poetry. How could such people who adorn a toxic medium like the movies, who undervalue even the nobler deeds of celluloid heroes like Buffalo Bill, would have known Tennyson and his poetry? The satire of the poem lies in this undercutting line.

The contrast between the splendour of Tennyson and the squalor of a cinema illustrate the corruption in contemporary values. Tennyson gave serious attention to the role of women in Victorian society, but the modern girl is paying homage to the "holy name" of Buffalo Bill and the climactic "bang! bang!" of the movies:

In the holy name bang! bang! the flowers came
With the marvellous touch of fingers
Gentler than the fuzzy goats
Moving up and down up and down as if in ecstasy
As the cowboys rode their skin-tight stallions
Over the barbarous hills of California.

In this poem, like his other poems, Smith sticks to his taciturnity and practises complete impersonality. Except for the speaker's undercutting, he remains as far off as possible from the poem.

Ode: The Eumenides (1942)

Eumenides is a Greek word meaning kind people. This poem needs to be read along with and as ironic commentary of "A Hyacinth for Edith." Where "Hyacinth" ends, the Eumenides ode begins. In the last lines of "Hyacinth," the poet yearns for a lost innocence:

And walk again the wild and sweet wildwood
Of our lost innocence, our ghostly childhood.

"Ode: The Eumenides" begins with the lines:

If we could go again
To the innocent wood
Where the crisp floor
Muffles the tread,
And the classic shade
Of cedar and pine
Soothes the depraved head

The desire to return to the "innocent wood" in the Eumenides ode is caused by a horrified recognition of the dead in the war. The poem shows a strong sense cf guilt on the part of the poet who longs for a return to the safety of a childhood free from responsibility. The easy comforts of religion and honour may not absolve one's guilt or his feeling of betrayal. Worldly prayer, however sincere and concentrated, has caused the destruction of the world and no one can escape:

The stench of the dead
Emptied and butchered hope
In lives and deaths made
Meaningless froth.

The last section of the poem is notable for its stock of stark imagery:

We have a date in another wood,
In the stifling dark,
Where the Furies are.

... ...

Where we spilled our bloodshot seed
They wait, each patient ghost
My ruined son.

Smith had originally used the compound noun "blood-begotten seed" which he later revised to "bloodshot seed" producing a pun (Michael Darling: "A.J.M. Smith", 257). The single word "bloodshot" avoids the artificiality of the compound noun while suggesting the inevitable violent death of the children emanating from such seed.

More than a satire on the ravages of war, this poem is an emotional poem of lamentation for the war-dead, like another of Smith's poem "The Soldier's Ghost."

From this brief discussion of Smith's social poems, we have understood that his satires are mild invectives lacking commitment. Desmond Pacey is right in stating that "the poems of social criticism of Smith are not the sincere expression of Smith's own convictions but a poser adopted because Auden had made it popular" (202) and "Smith's satires are inferior to that of F.R. Scott" (*The Ten Canadian Poets,* 208). However, such remarks might place Smith in disfavour. W.J. Keith makes a more balanced comparison of Scott and Smith. He writes:

Since Scott was far more directly concerned with social and political affairs than Smith, a much larger portion of his

> poetic output is devoted to satirical commentary on current affairs . . . while Smith was attracted to art through its promise of permanence. (*Canadian Literature in English,* 62)

Evidently, as commentaries on society, Smith's satirical poems are subtle and delicate. Though not forthright, Smith never lacked foresight.

5

In a Sort of Ecstasy: Smith's Exuberant Lyrics

Smith's poetic career is a wise balancing of joy and depressive visions, true to the spirit of the Santayana passage prefixed to his collection of poems *The Classic Shade*: "Every animal has his festive and ceremonious moments, when he poses or plumes himself or thinks; sometimes he even sings and flies aloft in a sort of ecstasy" (6). His love-lyrics and pastoral poetry embody his exuberant moments.

Since pastoralism remains a significant force in Smith's "festive" lyrics, it calls for a deeper understanding. In order to comprehend and evaluate his pastoral poetry it is essential to know the origin, development and important concepts of pastoral poetry. In classical literature, the pastoral was a convenient poetic form in which poets wrote about friends disguised as shepherds moving through rural landscape. During the classical revival in England in the seventeenth and eighteenth centuries, pastoral poetry was revived. Milton's *Lycidas* and Gray's *Elegy Written in a Country Churchyard* are notable adaptations of classical pastorals. Today the term pastoral is used to mean any poem of rural people and setting. Robert Frost, for example, is termed a pastoral poet by some critics. Since the classification in modern poetry is based on theme, rather than on form, it is not surprising that the term pastoral is used in association with other poetic types like the pastoral lyric, the pastoral drama and the pastoral epic.

Leo Marx's *The Machine in the Garden* is the most stimulating book on pastoralism and has become an accepted rubric in American literary criticism. For Marx, American literature is pastoral literature, and the American experience has been and still is a pastoral experience. He discusses in his book the broad changes made by machine technology on the pastoral ideal in America. However, our interest in Marx here is limited to an understanding of his pastoral concepts and not their application to America or American literature.

In Marx's approach, we find a more usable pastoralism. Pastoral literature, from Virgil's *Eclogues* to very recent narratives, has generally been considered a response to certain social problems. Marx defines the pastoral as "not just an art form [about social problems] but a mode of consciousness and itself a social problem – not just a matter of expression but of thought and behaviour" (5). He distinguishes between social or "sentimental pastoralism" and literary or "complex pastoralism." The mode of consciousness of sentimental pastoralism, according to Marx, is "a wish image of happiness" (24), or simply escapism. Complex pastoralism involves a "contrast of two conditions of consciousness," the tentative adoption of sentimental pastoralism as a life style and the eventual recognition of its impossibility. Marx contends that in complex pastoralism our experience is based on the "pastoral ideal" – the belief that man can live in a "middle landscape" situated between nature's primitivism and civilization's authority. But technology's power and progress are thwarting the actualization of this social theory, and industrialization has reduced the ideal to myth. The pastoral ideal, consequently, is an impracticable "mode of belief" yet a central part of the modern mind.

As a literary form, the pastoral is patterned on the traditional "pastoral design," a "redemptive journey" (69) away from society's problems into the wilderness and eventually back to civilization. And it has an important addition which Marx names the "interrupted idyll." By the term interrupted idyll, Marx means the shattering of the author's contemplation of a pastoral scene by a locomotive's shriek and transforming it into an awareness of urban and industrial power. The recurring image of the machine in the garden, shattering of the author's contemplation by the shrieking of the locomotive, then, is more than an aesthetic representation of disharmony. It is, in fact, a symptom of the social conflict between the pastoral ideal and the growth of technology.

Marx gives the example of *Adventures of Huckleberry Finn.* In Twain's novel, the garden is the raft, and the machine is the steamboat. The raft represents an escape from society, freedom from restriction, and a sense of plenty all associated with the pastoral idea. It "embraces all of the extravagant possibilities of sufficiency, spontaneity, and joy" (Marx, 330). The steamboat represents the intrusion of social realities into this dream. It is a representation of how machine technology conflicts the pastoral ideal. Marx identifies a tension between the two. This tension is expressed by the recurring image of the machine in the garden, that is, the repeated intrusion of technology into a pastoral scene. Marx writes:

> Within the lifetime of a single generation . . . a rustic and in large part wild landscape was transformed into the site of the world's most productive industrial machine. It would be difficult to imagine more profound contradictions of value or meaning than those made manifest by this circumstance. Its influence upon our literature is suggested by the recurrent image of the machine's sudden entrance into the landscape. (343)

Marx has given us such terms as "pastoral design," "sentimental pastoralism," "complex pastoralism" and "the interrupted idyll" which allow us to look deeper into the structure, emotions and conflicts in pastoral poetry in general. In the case of Canada, its literature is dominated by natural or small town settings, by images of the wilderness or rural life, and by a consciousness shaped by the experience of the land. Indeed, major Canadian writings were created out of a profound and pervasive awareness of the natural landscape. When human habitations appear in this literature, they are more often small towns than large cities. Whatever the reason for this tendency, whether the topographical fact or because there is something in the Canadian psyche that finds the city an uncongenial metaphor or landscape, it is a rural, rather than an urban, perspective that governs much of Canadian literature. However, in Canadian literature "complex pastoralism" predominates.

Smith, like Marx, was aware of the inadequacies and the complexities of the pastoral form in the age of industrial and technological advances and the possibility of its extinction. Hence, he attempted to revive the pastoral form in modern Canadian poetry but he was not a serious pastoralist. His pastoral poetry mainly serves an intertextual purpose. His lapidary poems were classical poems tempered with romanticism; his pastoral poems are personal poems tempered with classicism. "Ballade un Pue Banale," "An Iliad for His Summer Sweetheart," "A Pastoral," "Business as Usual 1946" and "The Country Lovers" are some of his pastoral lyrics.

Ballade un Pue Banale (1926)

"Ballade un Pue Banale" is an extreme expression of Santayana's phrase "in a sort of ecstasy." Rosenthal calls the poem a "parody of sexual melodrama with all the paraphernalia of medieval lyric, of pastoral romance, and of earthly piety." He finds in it "the simple sweetness of absurd erotic fantasy.. running twin risks of preciosity and vulgarity" (11). The poem is a lyric in the pastoral convention. It goes back to Rabelais and Chaucer and even earlier:

> The bellow of good Master Bull
> Astoundeth gentle Cow
> That standeth in the meadow cool
> Where cuckoo singeth now.
> She stoppeth in a moony trance
> Beneath the timeless trees
> While ebon-bellied shad-flies dance
> About her milk-white knees.

The poem is a parody, but in this poem the target of parody is not a particular author or a particular work but the style of a particular period. It has to be read as a light-hearted parody of the mediaeval lyrical and pastoral conventions. The essential features of a parody are present in the poem. The French title is in contrast with Anglo-Saxon archaisms such as

"Astoundeth," "singeth" and "standeth." There is a mishmash of the holy and the irreligious; for example, the infinity of God is given a limiting idea, when Christ is described as having to make use of "some miraculous device" to take the virgin cow to heaven:

I like to think sweet Jesus Christ,
For his dear mother's sake,
By some miraculous device,
Her to Himself did take;

That her preserv'd Virginity
Flutes holy flats and sharps
In that divine vicinity
Where Eliot's hippo harps.

The allusion to Eliot in the last line is unwarranted here. Edith Sitwell protests "the impertinence of using Mr. Eliot's name in such a context" (*Aspects of Modern Poetry,* 34). She rightly criticizes the poem as a "trivial and vulgar little blasphemy" (34).

Business as Usual 1946 (1946)

"Business as Usual" is a corporate pastoral. In traditional pastoral poetry, society is represented by the shepherds in a rural landscape. However, it is not always necessary to place shepherds in a bucolic environment. What is essential for pastoral poetry is rural/urban dialectic; pastoral poetry appears whenever the hustle and bustle of urban life grows hard to bear and people try to evade its pressures at least in thought. There are instances of pastoral poetry "where shepherds are replaced or represented by courtiers as in the Forest of Arden in Shakespeare's *As You Like It,* and mowers in Marvell's poetry" (Nageswara, Rao 131).

Smith's "Business as Usual 1946" extends the pastoral characters to the urban traders. Society is represented by the trading class in the poem. Nevertheless, Smith introduces delightful forests and flutes in the poem in order to meet the requirements of the traditional pastoral mode:

In this delightful forest, fluted so,
We burghers of the sunny central plain
Fable a still refuge from the spears
That clank – but gently clank – but clank again!

The delightful forest is troubled by "the spears / that clank." The word "clank" repeated three times in this stanza is a referent for the agony of urban life. It connects to the "clank" in the first stanza:

Across the craggy indigo
Come rumours of the flashing spears
And in the clank of rancid moon
There is a tone, and such a tone.

Obviously, the safety of life in the woods is threatened by the "flashing spears" of urban living. The "clank of rancid moon" imagery presents the commotion of urban life which is in conflict with the quiet life of the "protecting bosks":

How tender! How insidious!
The air grows gentle with protecting bosks,
And furry leaves take branch and root
Here we are safe, we say, and slyly smile.

Smith looks at urban life with irony. The words "insidious" and "slyly" are suggestive of the scepticism of Smith. To the "delightful forest" and "furry leaves," Smith has added the shadow of doubt and has become an "urban pastoralist" (Leo Marx, 49). By his realistic presentations, Smith has related pastoral conventions to contemporary social issues.

Brigadier (1948)

"Brigadier," translated from a French-Canadian song, is not a pastoral poem, but one of Smith's light-humoured exuberant lyrics. It is romantic in its music of opposing tones and at the same time remarkably impersonal. The poem is in the form of a nagging dialogue between a proud general and his mockingly respectful sergeant, Pandore. The first stanza introduces the pair:

One Sunday morning soft and fine
Two old campaigners let their nags meander;
One was a Sergeant of the Line,
The other a Brigade Commander.
The General spoke with martial roar,
'Nice weather for this time of year!'
And 'Right you are,' replied Pandore,
'Right you are, my Brigadier.'

In the following stanzas, the Brigadier's superior romanticism ironically juxtaposes with the sergeant's cold, unconcerned impassiveness.

'I have gathered Glory's laurel
With the rose of Venus twined –
I am Married, and a General;
Yet, by Jesus, I've a mind
To start like Jason for the golden shore
And follow my star – away from here!'
'Ah, right you are,' replied Pandore,
'Right you are, my Brigadier.'

So runs the dialogue. The language of the loquacious Brigadier slowly becomes bombastic and pretentious, but the sergeant is restrained and unconcerned throughout. In the final stanzas, the narrator takes over the general's style and parodies it mockingly and Pandore repeats his refrain mecha ically:

They rode in silence for a while:
You only heard the measured tread
Of muffled hoof beats, mile on mile –
But when Aurora, rosy red,
Unbarred her eastern door,
The faint refrain still charmed the ear,
As 'Right you are,' replied Pandore,
'Right you are, my Brigadier.'

Can there be a better piece of absurdity? The two characters, Brigadier and Pandore, are a happy discovery. The sergeant's chorus-like refrain continues eternally. The poem is a finest piece of social parody.

What the Emanation of Casey Jones Said to the Medium (1957)

"What the Emanation of Casey Jones Said to the Medium" and "What is That Music High in the Air?" are companion poems concerned with the theme of death. They discuss death not in a serious, metaphysical vein but in a droll acceptance of death as an essential part of life. It is because of this cheerful attitude to mortality these poems have been grouped with Smith's other poems of exuberance.

The poem is in the railroaders' jargon. It is in eight stanzas of rhyming quatrains. The first quatrain establishes the link between the predominant images of the poem, the functioning of the brain and the mechanism of the train:

> Turn inward on the brain
> The flashlight of an I,
> While the express train
> Time, unflagged, roars by.

The poem, like the Canadian folk-singer Casey Jones' folk-songs, as the title suggests, is a vibrant combination of conversational language and lively music in the elegiac tone. It associates the death-feelings of the railroaders' with the grimmer reality of the mechanical power and speed of the engine:

> Then shine, O curdled orb,
> Within thy vantage box,
> Field that attracts, absorbs
> Cats, hairpins, spring greens, clocks,
>
> That twists like vapour, seeps
> From tunnel's murky bung
> Hole, fogs the vista-dome and creeps
> Away, accomplished and undone.

Mind is described as the "Field that attracts" everything good and bad. The last quatrain which repeats the first-line of the first quatrain winds up the poem:

Turn inward to the brain:
The signal stars are green,
Unheard the ghost train
Time and Death cannot be seen.

Time and Death, like ghost trains, are unpredictable; they need to be acknowledged and accepted whole-heartedly when the "signal stars are green." The atypical spacing between "can" and "not" in the last line suggests that perception or spiritual attainment is a rare and fortunate event.

To Donne, air was the "medium" though which the spirit was conveyed to the mind; but Smith, through related images of train, exhaust and fog, has developed a modern concept to convey the spirit to the mind. In Smith's poem, the narrator is fortunate because the mind intervenes and attainment is possible.

What is That Music High in the Air? (1957)

The title of the poem, "What is that Music High in the Air?" is a line from Eliot's poem *The Waste Land.* It is a sentimental poem paying homage to "the inconsequential dead." It is also one of the noblest efforts of Smith's high lyrical evocation in an exalted mood:

A voice from the heroic dead,
Unfaltering and clear,
Rings from the overhead
And zips into the ear;

The phrase "Unfaltering and clear" contrasts with "He asks of heart / To bear a braver part" in the poem "Journey" where the poet is in the grips of fear of death, whereas, here, he is bold and fearless to face death. The lines:

And tomorrow will be late,
For the ear will turn to clay
And the scrannel pipe will grate,
Shiver, and die away

describing the body decaying to shreds and new life emerging from the shreds are concerned with reductive metamorphosis of death. The poem ends, however, with lamentation and sympathy for the humble-dead:

> A sigh of the inconsequential dead,
> A murmur in a drain,
> Lapping a severed head,
> Unlaurelled, unlamented, vain.

Smith arrives at this conclusion by evolving a process of contemplation and correction which is against the poem's lofty opening lines.

A Pastoral (1958)

The poem that very clearly shows Smith's attitude to pastoral poetry is his poem entitled "A Pastoral." Its earlier title was "Variations on a Theme of Cavalcanti." Its adaptation from Cavalcanti's "Ballata IX" suggests its classical reference. The poem illustrates Smith's manipulation of classical pastoral conventions. Cavalcanti's poem is a "true-blue" traditional pastoral, but Smith's poem combines the traditional with the modern. Smith creates a world of shepherds, woods and benign nature very much in the traditional mode; but he introduces these elements only to question the propriety of the application of the pastoral ideals of spontaneity, innocence, and piety to the coarseness of the modern world. In Cavalcanti the shepherd experiences a sense of inner harmony from which is derived our awareness of the spirit of fulfilment in all created things; in Smith this awareness is undercut by the psyche of the poet.

The words "I wonder," "I dreamed" and "I said within my heart" (note the frequency of occurrence of 'I' here which is in contrast with his early poems where he says "I am not I") suggest the egotistic state of mind of the shepherd. Smith's poem begins:

> I wandered in a little wood, and there
> I met a shepherdess. So fair
> She seemed, I dreamed
> She were a moonbeam, a fountain, or a star.

The corresponding lines in the translation of Cavalcanti read:

> In wood-way found I once a shepherdess,
> More fair than stars are was she to my seeming

The following two quatrains, which describe the shepherdess and her state of mind, blends nature with sensuality beautifully:

> Her cheeks were white and red,
> And with a wand her sheep she led.
> The cold dew wet her pretty twinkling feet.
> O love O love O love, she said.
>
> Heart-touched, I did reply,
> And gently asked her why
> She walked alone, and made her plaintive moan
> To stocks and stones, green trees, and the blue sky.

When the "cold dew" falls on her pretty feet she becomes rapturous and makes whispers of love in her "plaintive moan." The refreshing influence of the shepherd is observed in another stanza:

> When I hear the small bird sing
> And see the flutter of his speckled wing
> My heart turns over. I long for a lover
> In the greenwood in early spring.

When he hears the song of the bird and sees it flutter, his heart overflows with love like that of the shepherdess in the earlier stanzas. It is the benign nature that brings harmony to the shepherd and the shepherdess.

In contrast to the sensual description of the shepherdess in the first quatrain of the poem, she is condemned in the final lines:

> She was no moonbeam, star, or dream,
> Nor icy changing crystal stream
> But very woman, such (I say) as no man
> Might not love, nor her misdeem.

The translation of the relevant passage in "Ballata IX" is given below:

> She held to me with a dear wilfulness
> Saying her heart had gone into my bosom,
> She drew me on to a cool leafy place
> When I got sight of every coloured blossom,
> And there I drank in so much summer sweetness
> Me seemed Love's god connived at its completeness.

Cavalcanti's poem ends with the fulfilment of desire: his garden is not interrupted by the machine. In Smith's poem, it is different. The fulfilment of desire is undercut by the realization that the shepherdess is after all an ordinary woman ("a very woman"), who need not be adorned with sacred pastoral appellations.

The Country Lovers (1958)

"The Country Lovers" is an eclogue with the subtitle "A Little Eclogue for Irving and Aviva." The poem is a lampoon against another Canadian poet Irving Layton. Smith wrote the poem because of the differences he had with *First Statement* group of which Layton was a prominent member. Smith has written some more poems offending Layton like "On Reading Certain Poems of Irving Layton and Louis Dudek," "To Irving Layton on His passion for the First Lady" and "On Reading Layton's Poetry as the Fine Art of Pugilism." "Smith's contributions to this controversy are characterized by wit and delicacy, and an eighteenth century elegance that Layton cannot, and does not try to match" (Woodcock: "A.J.M. Smith", 263).

In this poem, to ensure that .the readers comprehend the target of attack, Smith has mentioned "Irving" in the subtitle and "Layton" in the text. The poem is also critical of the application of the sacred pastoral convention to the sexuality of the modern society. The poem is in three couplets:

> A solemn stillness fills the sacred grove
> Where Layton and his sweet Aviva love:

Rabbits, rank goats, and ruffled sparrows stare
In envious admiration – and despair

While Venus, wandering by to bless the place,
Feels a pure blush suffuse her conscious face.

The pastoral convention emphasizes the instinct for love as the sacred principle of life. But "rank goats" and "ruffled sparrows" in the poem are suggestive of incest; these images do not describe the celestial love of traditional pastorals but the crude sexuality of the modern world. By making use of pastoral material in this poem, Smith subverts sacrilegious use of the pastoral ideal of love.

An eclogue is a short pastoral poem, usually in dialogue, on the subject of rural life and the society of shepherds, showing it as an escape from the complexity and corruption of civilization. One type of classical eclogue is a singing match where two shepherds sing for a prize, with a third shepherd acting as judge. In this poem, the three couplets correspond to the three stages. In the first couplet, Smith describes Layton and Aviva in the "sacred grove." In terms of the singing match analogy, Layton makes his claim of Aviva:

A solemn stillness fills the sacred grove
Where Layton and his sweet Aviva love;

The descriptive adjectives "solemn," "sacred" and "sweet" are suggestive of divinity. The unforced naturalness in the alveolar sound in "solemn stillness," "sacred" and "sweet" are symbolic of the ideal.

In the second couplet, in terms of the match analogy, rabbits, goats and sparrow compete against Layton for Aviva. There is also a depiction of libidinous love:

Rabbits, rank goats, and ruffled sparrows stare
In envious admiration – and despair;

This stanza is in an altogether different tone from the first stanza. "Rank," "ruffled," "envious," "despair" and "stare" are in contrast with the solemn adjectives of the first stanza and are suggestive of greediness, envy and frustration.

In the third couplet, Venus sitting in judgment feels aggrieved:

> While Venus, wandering by to bless the place,
> Feels a pure blush suffuse her conscious face.

The poem is different from classical pastorals in that there is no harmony between the lovers and the objects of nature because the objects of nature "stare" and "blush" at the earthly lovers.

An Iliad for His Summer Sweetheart (1963)

In "An Iliad for His Summer Sweetheart" a classical reference from Ezra Pound's *Homage to Sextus Propertius* is used as epigraph. The poet is conceptualizing an Iliad for his sweetheart who so charmingly lets his imagination wander over meadowlands of erotic fancy:

> I love to see my Amaryllis toss her shirt
> Away and kick her panties off, and loll,
> Languid and lazy, by the lily pool,
> While old Silenus leers and laughing Cupids squirt.
>
> My fancies swarm like bees about her golden head
> And golden thighs, where love's best ore is found.
> When she sinks softly to the sun-warmed ground
> We need no silken walls, no blinds, no feather bed.

In "An Iliad," Smith indulges in romantic extremes calling into reference the mythological figures Amaryllis, Silenus and Cupid. The phrases "golden head" and "golden thighs" have a classical allusion: "golden" suggests eternity and timelessness. As such, the poem, more than erotic, describes innocent pleasure. Rosenthal writes:

> It's hard to think of another contemporary who takes such innocent pleasure in innocent pleasure as Smith does but just out of glee such things can be.
>
> ("Introduction": *The Classical Shade* 17)

The poem is made sensuous by the use of tactile images like "softly," "silken" and "sun-warmed ground." The warmth of the poem barring the ironic intent, recalls Keats' description of Madeline in *The Eve of St. Agnes:*

> . . . her vespers done,
> Of all its wreathed pearls her hair she frees;
> Unclasps her warmed jewels one by one;
> Loosens her fragrant bodice; by degrees
> Her rich attire creeps rustling to her knees:
> Half-hidden, like a mermaid in sea-weed,
> Pensive awhile she dreams awake. (226-32)

In its classical references and description of romantic melancholy, the poem resembles Bliss Carman's translation of the lost lyrics of the Greek poetess, Sappho. Two of the surviving *Sappho* fragments read:

> I loved thee, Atthis, in the long ago.
> When the great oleanders were in flower
> In the broad herded meadows full of sun.
>
> . . .   .
>
> Softer than the hill-fog to the forest
> Are the loving hands of my dear lover,
> When she sleeps beside me in the starlight
> And her beauty drenches me with rest.
> (Quoted in W. J. Keith: *Canadian Literature in English* 36)

The diction of "An Iliad" is classical with tight, conventional versification. The poem is made of two quatrains of interlocked rhyme pattern with two hexameter lines sandwiching two pentameter lines.

Souvenirs du Temps Perdu (1966)

"Souvenirs du Temps Perdu" is a light-hearted exercise in drinking. It is a pastiche on epicurean and Bacchanalian revelry which Smith has written for his friend, Leon Edel.

A pastiche is a literary genre that is either a "hodgepodge" or an "imitation." As a hodgepodge, a pastiche is "cobbled together" in duplication of several original works. This meaning is in accord with its etymology. *Pastiche* is the French version of the Italian dish *pasticcio*, which is a kind of pie made of many different ingredients. As an imitation, a pastiche denotes a literary technique employing a generally light-hearted tongue-in-cheek imitation of another's style. Although jocular, it is usually respectful. Frederic Jameson describes a pastiche as "blank parody" (72) especially with reference to the postmodern parodic practices of self-reflexivity and intertextuality.

Smith's poem "Souvenirs du Temps Perdu" is a hodgepodge of innumerable literary sources though the dominant source is that of T.S. Eliot. The poem begins:

> The champignon salad has repeated
> to the verge of tedium.
> We sit in the Dome
> to the ditto of *le meme*
> as French as a French fried potato
> in a greasy cornucopia
> of the *Montreal Daily Star.*

The lines refer to a cornucopia of mushroom salad and French fried potato: an abundant, uninterrupted supply of food and drinks. The lines are reminiscent of the characteristic description of Hemingway of cafe-life in his war-time novel *The Sun Also Rises* set in Spain.

There is crude humour in the lines:

> I will arise and go now
> and go to the lavabo
> where men without women
> are standing in a row.

The line "I will arise and go now" is from Yeats' poem, "The Lake Isle of Innisfree." "Men without Women" is, again, the title of Hemingway's collection of short stories. The following lines:

God I will rise and take a train
and get me to April once again
for April is the cruellest nymph
scattering garters and spent stays
on an unmade bed in a one-room head.

These lines form a patchwork of the opening lines of *The Waste Land* and a few other lines in "The Fire Sermon" section of the same poem. *The Waste Land* opens with the following lines:

April is the cruellest month, breeding
Lilacs out of the dead land, mixing
Memory and desire, stirring
Dull roots with spring rain.

In Smith's line ". . . April is the cruellest nymph," April is not the month but name of a girl and "nymph" is euphemism for a prostitute as in the opening lines of "The Fire Sermon" section of *The Waste Land* which is in itself a parody of Spenser's "Prothalamion":

The river's tent is broken: the last fingers of leaf
Clutch and sink into the wet bank. The wind
Crosses the brown land, unheard. The nymphs are departed.
Sweet Thames, run softly, till I end my song.

The images of "garters" and "spent stays" are again from "The Fire Sermon." The corresponding lines in "The Fire Sermon" read:

Out of the window perilously spread
Her drying combinations touched by the sun's last rays
On the divan are piled (at night her bed)
Stockings, slippers, camisoles, and stays.

The next two lines in the poem involve direct quotation:

O to be in April now that
Yes sir she's my baby . . . .

The first line is from Robert Browning's "Home Thoughts from Abroad." The second line is from a popular song. These lines undercut the earlier references to April by, "Yes sir she's my baby." The final lines:

> Would you mind not forgetting
> to leave something in the bowl
> as you
> pass out

are Smith's own and are in the manner of a non-sequiter employed by Smith to shift the point of view from the apparent content of the poem.

Smith's imitative virtuosity has helped him to concoct a new poem out of familiar phrases and citations. In this way, he has prefigured a powerful postmodern mode of satire.

Obviously light verse was of special interest to Smith in his middle career. In 1951, he compiled an important anthology of light verse entitled *The Worldly Muse.* He wrote an article on light verse for the *Princeton Encyclopaedia of Poetry and Poetics.* In it he defines the characteristics of light verse as "a tough reasonableness beneath the slight lyric grace" (448). He defines "Tough reasonableness" as an absence of "squeamishness, hard-headedness, good sense, intelligence, a sense of values, a rational worldliness." He defines "slight lyrical grace" as "verbal excellence, technical accomplishment, perfect and economical adaptation of means to an end." The definition aptly describes Smith's own efforts in light verse in such poems as "Souvenirs du Temps Perdu," "Brigadier" and "An Iliad for His Summer Sweetheart."

These love-lyrics, along with the pastorals and pastiche which he wrote in a sort of ecstasy, led to a revaluation of his poetry. They diverted critical attention from stereotyping Smith as a classical, metaphysical poet. Milton Wilson praises Smith's "energetic and life-enhancing qualities" (16). Louis Dudek writes: "Smith's austere poetics are balanced with life-affirming realism" ("Aesthetic Master of Canadian Poetry" 13). Smith has proved himself to be an energetic, exuberant poet in these poems.

6

To Be Nothing is to Be All: Smith's Poems on Death

In our analysis of the imagist poems of Smith, we saw that perception led to assessment. We also saw that the quality of assessment in each poem was different. Smith accomplished this by modifying the default imagist practices. Similarly, in his poems on death, there is progress from fear of death to understanding of death. Smith achieves this by making essential changes in the seventeenth century metaphysical practices.

Acknowledging the presence of metaphysical elements in Smith's poetry, Sandra Djwa calls him a "modern metaphysical" ("Of Metaphysics and Dry Bones", 29). She observes that Smith's knowledge of the seventeenth century metaphysical poetry is shaped partly by "Eliot's discovery of certain qualities of technique and sensibility in the poetry of the early seventeenth century" (29). Smith doubtless is indebted to Eliot for his modernism and "certain qualities of technique." But, in the shaping of Smith's metaphysical mind, Eliot has a very limited part. When Heenan asked Smith where he would place Eliot among those whom he was vitally concerned with, Smith's reply was cold and unconcerned. He said: "I always placed Eliot very highly, read him with great delight and pleasure – particularly the early poems" (Heenan: online).

There are other strong and reliable sources for Smith's metaphysical observations. While Smith was on a fellowship at the University of Edinburgh, his tutorials with H.J.C. Grierson, who had already brought out an edition of metaphysical poetry, sharpened his interest in the seventeenth century metaphysical poets. Smith's doctoral thesis was on *Studies in the Metaphysical Poets of the Anglican Church in the Seventeenth Century.* During this time he read plenty of Vaughan, Herbert and Donne and was inspired by them in that order. Yet another source of metaphysical influence on Smith was in his Neo-Platonic approach. Neo-Platonism held that all existence, material and spiritual, emanated from a transcendent One through the divine mind and world soul; freedom from sin could be gained by the individual soul only by seeking reintegration with the One. Smith insists upon this principle in almost all his poems on death in their "Nothing-All" juxtapositions. Smith's metaphysical poetry is, then, in addition to Eliot, an effective combination of Vaughan's mysticism and Renaissance Neo-Platonism. The love of paradox and hyperbole, the fusion of the intellectual and colloquial diction, and an insistence on the tough logic beneath a lyric grace of romantic experience characterize his new-metaphysical poetry.

Conflict has always been the subject-matter of Smith's poetry. There is the conflict of elements like wind against tree, water against stone, spray against sky in his imagist poetry. The opposition between real and false, ideal past and tawdry present is the subject-matter of his pastorals and social satires. Similarly, the divergence between Nothing-All, life-in-death and death-in-life is the content of his poems on death.

The theme of fear of death and its recognition in rebirth is also the major theme of Leo Kennedy, a friend and follower of Smith. In his collection *The Shrouding* Kennedy presents a sequence of life which consists of the ecstasy of sexual love, the horror of death and the mystery of resurrection. When he thinks of love he usually thinks of death; and when he thinks of death he always thinks of resurrection. A similar pattern is found in Smith's poems also. The two were concerned with Vaughan's poetic use of the myth of day in night and night in day.

Smith and Vaughan also share similarity of form. Vaughan's poems generally follow a tripartite structure consisting of meditative act, analysis and discussion in the style of Renaissance meditation literature. A similar pattern is found in Smith's poems.

Journey (1926)

This discussion of Smith's metaphysical poems on death – the voyage from fear of death to recognition of death – very interestingly starts with a poem titled "Journey." It was first published in 1926. It was revised and published again in 1928. The revised version is discussed here because it is the text which Smith intended.

The easiest and the best way to summarize this poem is citing the first two lines of Dryden's *Mac Flecknoe*:

> All human things are subject to decay,
> And when fate summons monarchs must obey.

"Journey" is a very simple poem expressing the poet's morbid fear of death and its inescapability. The theme is treated in two sections of eight lines each. The first three lines set the tone of the poem:

> One and by one
> Under a drooping sun
> His footsteps fall.

The poet is journeying alone to an unknown destination. While describing his journey, Smith makes use of very popular images. Associating death with night has always been the convention. Hence he makes use of the imagery of "drooping sun." But in his later poems, it will be seen that night and death have positive connotation. The next five lines read:

> With heavy tread
> And unbowed head
> He goes alone
>
> The end unknown,
> On either hand a wall.

Loneliness ("He goes alone") is emphasized throughout in the poem. A "wall" is a polypody suggestive of lonely, melancholic wandering. Matthew Arnold's scholar-gypsy was seen to:

> . . . stray
> Rapt, twirling in thy hand a withered spray
> And waiting for the spark from heaven to fall.

Similarly, Smith's narrator is shown as holding a wall-cress in each hand. The next three lines read:

> Death walks behind
> With pace designed
> An overtaking tread.

Death is shown as dominant of the two by the phrase "pace designed" and the participle "overtaking." The rhyme and the rhythm show Death's determined pace. It is imminent for Death to overtake in this journey, yet the poet,

> He asks of heart
> To bear a braver part
> When death draws nigh
>
> And for reply,
> Heart moveth not. And all is said.

These lines describe Smith's intense fear of death and express his fineness of sensibility.

Smith has used powerfully the journey motif to communicate the idea of life and death. The two versions of the poem will enable us to see how his revisions have transformed it from a clumsy, romantic and diffuse poem to a modern classic.

In line 10 of the first version ("One comes behind"), Death is a possible meaning for "One." This is made specific in the second version. But the most significant change involves depersonalization – the elimination of the first person pronoun and the substitution of the third person singular "He."

The two versions are given below to show the full range of alterations:

1926 Version	1928 Version
One and by one Under the drooping sun My footsteps fall.	One and by one Under a drooping sun His footsteps fall.
With unbowed head	With heavy tread And heavy tread
And unbowed head	I go alone, He goes alone,
The end unknown, On either hand a wall.	The end unknown, On either hand a wall.
In the cold wind One comes behind With overtaking tread.	Death walks behind With pace designed – An overtaking tread.
I ask my heart To bear a braver part When he draws nigh.	He asks of heart To bear a braver part When Death draws nigh:
Heart whispers, "Aye". No other word is said.	And for reply – Heart moveth not. And all is said.

It is in line 12 that this revision is most deeply felt, where the possessive pronoun "my" is omitted altogether in the *second version*. The omission of the pronoun serves an important purpose – it increases the objectivity of the experience by placing the heart outside the control of the poet. In the first version, "Heart" accedes to the speaker's request "To bear a braver part / When he draws nigh." But the revised stanza is far more profound in its acceptance of death. When "He asks of heart" the same thing in the revised poem, the "Heart moveth not. And all is said."

Because Smith has eliminated the possessive pronoun to let the heart stand on its own, he is, in effect, underlining the inability of the poet to control his own destiny. The earlier imagery supports this conclusion. The sun is "drooping," Death is overtaking him. With his head unbowed, the poet asks the heart to tell what it can do for him at such a critical moment. But the heart has nothing to say (Michael Darling: "A.J.M. Smith's Revision to His Poems", 13).

The Two Sides of a Drum (1926)

Having known that death is inescapable, Smith yearns for eternity in "The Two Sides of a Drum":

> When Night lets down her hair
> Over the pale blossom
> Of the world, far, far from here
> With sealed eyes, still bosom
> And folded feet I fare
> To that country under dream
> Where eternity and time
> Are the two sides of a drum.

The poem reflects Yeats's "Sailing to Byzantium" where the poet sails the seas and comes to the holy city of Byzantium and proclaims: "gather me / Into the artifice of eternity." The personification of "Night" as a goddess who "lets down her hair / Over the pale blossom of the world" is sensuous. The personification has many connotations. For Vaughan, Night was the time of spirits, the time when man could best approach his God:

> O for that Night! Where I in Him
> Might live invisible and dim!

The phrases "sealed eyes" and "still bosom" in the poem are also suggestive of death. The poet's yearning for eternity represents his angst to escape the pangs of death.

Prothalamium (1928)

"Prothalamium" describes the horrors of death. Though "Prothalamium" is a marriage verse, Smith has employed images suggesting horror, nausea, hysteria and monstrousness in the poem because it is the marriage of Death that is celebrated. The poem is in the Elizabethan lyric tradition, the setting is Victorian, the theme is metaphysical and the manner is modern.

The whole world of literature is involved in the allusions of the poem. The effect is to extend the power of evil of death to universal dimensions. The title recalls Spenser's poem by the same title. The first four lines have possible allusions to Tennyson and Hopkins:

> Here in this narrow room there is no light;
> The dead tree sings against the window pane;
> Sand shifts a little, easily; the wall
> Responds a little, inchmeal, slowly, down.

The comma after each word in the last-line represents "inchmeal" action. The fifth line, "My sister, whom my dust shall marry" is a reference to Rossetti's "My Sister's Sleep." The following lines recall Eliot:

> Consummation ushered in
> By wind in sundry corners.

References to Webster's *Duchess of Malfi* and Shakespeare's *Hamlet* follow:

> This holy sacrament was solemnized
> In harsh poetics a good while ago –
> At Malfy and the Danish battlements.

The marriage which is celebrated in the battle-field in harsh poetics suggests an ironic, topsy-turvy reality and reminds us of the Chorus in Eliot's *Murder in the Cathedral* which is "United to the spiritual flesh of nature, mastered by the animal powers of spirit." The situation is one of pervasive disorder in the natural world. The music of the last three lines has no equal:

> Tree fumbling pane, bell tolling,
> Ceiling dripping and the plaster falling,
> And Death, the voluptuous, calling.

The figures of the first stanza are repeated here with imagistic precision: "The dead tree sings against the window pane" has become "Tree fumbling pane"; "the wall / Responds a little" has become "the plaster falling." Not only the literary world, but the whole earth trembles over the marriage of Death. All sense of time and place are lost and the immensity of cosmic evil overwhelms. The poem clearly illustrates the hallucinatory fear that death has produced on the poet.

We might infer that Smith is celebrating "the union of Eros and Thanatos" because the last line "And Death, the voluptuous calling" (Sandra Djwa: "Of Metaphysics and Dry Bones", 24). However, Eros, who marries Thanatos, is also worshipped as God of Fertility. This knowledge might incidentally lead us to the understanding that Smith deviates from the seventeenth century metaphysical concepts about soul and spirit in this poem. The decay of the body, which for Donne and Vaughan signified the return of the soul to God, is reinterpreted by Smith. His understanding is based on the concept of the fertility myth as outlined by James Frazer. Obviously, the marriage of Thanatos (Death) to Eros (God of Fertility) is a step ahead in Smith's journey motif as there is hint of a resolution in the fertility myths for the problem of life and death.

The Archer (1937)

"The Archer" has to be compared with "The Two Sides of a Drum." In "The Two Sides of the Drum" Smith yearns for eternity after death. In "The Archer" he wants to overcome death by the immortality of art. "The Archer" was chosen by Smith to conclude his last book of poems *The Classical Shade.* Smith tells on the uniqueness of the poem in an article:

> 'The Archer' is not the only poem that the ambivalent and very oppressive feeling about death led, or rather forced, me to write; but it is the only one that was traditional or academic in form and diction. ("The Poetic Process": *Towards a View,* 227)

In the article, Smith recalls his attempts to begin a poem on death with echoes of Shelley and Longfellow in his mind, and the mental image of an arrow in the sky. By a laborious process, involving, he says, twenty or more drafts, he completed the first four and a half lines. The next three and a half, the sentence beginning "Then, loosening, fling . . ." came a good deal more easily. Smith then goes on to describe the composition of the sestet of the poem.

Clearly the poem is a fine statement of his belief and a good example of his craftsmanship. It is a Petrarchan sonnet. A sonnet is a lyrical poem of fourteen lines. The Petrarchan also called the Italian, regular or classical sonnet, is divided into the octave (first eight lines) and the sestet (last six lines). The octave has the rhyme scheme *abba abba*; the sestet has the rhyme scheme *cde cde*. A sonnet expresses in condensed form one feeling, one idea, or one emotion.

"The Archer" is a poem dealing with the universal problem of life and death, and life is imagined as an arrow. The arrow is an archetypal symbol. In this poem, Smith's arrow, like Donne's "flea" and Blake's "sick rose," assumes added significance. The octave is descriptive. The first quatrain of the octave describes the archer bending the bow and releasing the arrow into the empty sky:

> Bend back thy bow, O Archer, till the string
> Is level with thine ear, thy body taut,
> Its nature art, thyself thy statue wrought
> Of marble blood, thy weapon the poised wing
> Of coiled and aquiline Fate.

Thus far everything is static. The bow is bent back; the archer is poised in a statuesque position; the arrow is aimed. Now the coiled spring should be released and the arrow allowed flying in its path. The internal rhyme in "body taut . . . nature art . . . statue wrought" is very pleasing and illustrative of the musical qualities of Smith.

In the next quatrain of the octave, the aimed arrow is loosened to hit the target:

> . . . Then, loosening, fling
> The hissing arrow like burning thought
> Into the empty sky that smokes as the hot
> Shaft plunges to the bullseye's quenching ring.

The sestet is a one-line sentence which describes the arrow returning to the "targeted grave":

> Into the heart of what I know and hate –
> That central black, the ringed and targeted grave.

The poet does not await his death. He takes life into his hands in the form of an arrow and launches an attack on death. The arrow comes back to earth. The poet now learns that it is by his art that he has to defeat death. "The Archer," thus, emphasizes the power of art to overcome death.

To Henry Vaughan (1931)

Smith wrote "To Henry Vaughan" as a tribute to Grierson. He presented the poem to Grierson along with his doctoral dissertation *Studies in the Metaphysical Poets of the Anglican Church in the Seventeenth Century*. Later he revised and published it as a tribute to Henry Vaughan in *The Tamarack Review* in 1959. The poem is in heroic couplets in the fashion of eighteenth century popular verse during which time Vaughan lived.

Smith was closer to Herbert and Vaughan in the choice of his metaphysical concepts. Herbert was among the greatest writers of poems on sacred subjects. His poems show his zeal for the Church of England and are concerned with practical theology. He describes his poems as "a picture of the many spiritual conflicts that have passed between God and my soul, before I could subject mine to the will of Jesus my Master; in whose service I have now found perfect freedom" (Wikipaedia: online). His poems are marked with a note of devotion and simplicity. It is the simplicity of Herbert that is the secret of his power.

Influenced by Herbert, Vaughan experienced a religious conversion and wrote religious and mystical poetry on man and his relation to God. Vaughan was not a priest like Herbert but a mystic at heart. He was more at home in sacred than in secular verse. He had a considerable gift of fantasy. He is at his best when he deals with the themes of communion with nature and with eternity. His poem "The Retreat" influenced

Wordsworth in the composition of his *Intimations Ode*. Like Wordsworth, Vaughan saw God in nature. His poem "The World" contains the following popular lines:

> I saw eternity the other night
> Like a great ring of pure and endless light
> All calm as it was right.

In Smith's poetic journey from death-fear to death-recognition "To Henry Vaughan" is a landmark. For the first time recognition is indicated in "Nothing-All" juxtaposition appearing in the poem.

Smith presents in crisp and decisive manner Vaughan's longing for eternity, his homestead, in the opening stanza:

> Homesick? and yet your country walks
> Were heaven'd for you. Such bright stalks
> Of grasses! such pure Green! such blue
> Clear skies! such light! such silver dew! –

The lines echo Vaughan's lyric and mimetic sweetness. The opening line has direct reference to Vaughan's "He heaven'd for you" in his poem "The Search." Smith has used wisely images from Vaughan's poems "Regeneration," "The World," "and "The Night" in these lines:

> Celestial strings might not surpass
> Thy morning breezes in long grass;
> The slow rain from the laden tree,
> Dropping from heaven, brought to thee
> Sounds of the purest harmony,
> Setting thy caged soul free to fly.

It shows through a series of analogies that nature, because of being infused by God, is heaven on earth. The lines have a natural movement expressing Vaughan's going other-worldliness and Smith's unrestricted openness in description of nature.

The religious paradox with which the poem ends is both a declaration and recognition:

> Thou art content to beg a pall,
> Glad to be Nothing, to be All.

Behind Vaughan's joyful anticipation to be "Nothing" is the seventeenth century metaphysical concept; behind Smith's philosophic "All" is the Neo-Platonic doctrine of all existence springing from the transcendent One through the divine mind and world soul. Smith had prefigured this recognition in the "Nothing-All" paradox in the "nothing" of "The Creek." It will recur in Smith's poems on regeneration.

An existing debate over whether the poem respects or ridicules Vaughan has to be resolved. In the lines:

> Lifting the rapt soul out of Time
> Into a long Eternity

the phrase "long Eternity" is considered by some critics to be ironic, and, if irony was intended by Smith, it has to be a ridicule. Smith has the reply:

> Its purpose . . . is not to be ironic at the expense of the naivete of Henry Vaughan. Far from it . . . I think this gets across for the reader who is sympathetic to Vaughan or to Christian or Platonic ideas. . . . For one who is not, the effect of irony does come through after all, and gently indicates the noble futility of Vaughan's magnificent piety." ("A Self-Review": *Towards a View,* 215-16)

As "To Henry Vaughan" was written earlier and revised later, and the important concluding lines were inserted during one of the revisions, they do not fit into the integral structure of the poem. But other fine poems on death which Smith wrote later are unified by a more personal approach and colloquial diction, a simpler and more genuine fusion of thought and emotion.

"On Knowing *Nothing*" describes death in the context of horrors of death. "Watching the Old Man Die" describes sickly fear over his death. "My Death" is a poem where Smith is waiting for his own death. These poems develop the "Glad to be Nothing" scheme of Smith in a subtle way.

On Knowing *Nothing* (1956)

In its description of fear of death, "On Knowing *Nothing*" contrasts with "Journey," where the apprehension of a man about to die was the subject of discussion. Here the speaker is cognizant of the horrors of death but contemplates over it because:

> I cannot let the hollow
> Interval alone.

The language is colloquial and alliterative giving the poem a very popular rhythm:

> Out of this savoury fatness I
> Should suck the sharp surmise
> That strangles dying eyes

The alliteration in "Should suck the sharp surmise / That strangles" is natural and superb. Although death wants to grow, the body that houses it recoils in fear. Science ("surgeon's jab") and sex ("a woman's thigh") can give only temporary relief from the fear of death:

> The surgeon's jab, a woman's thigh,
> Give blank surcease
> For short or long.

Escape from fear of death is possible only by dying:

> As deep, as nothing, as the grave.

Apart from the romantic rhythm and humane description, the metaphysical thoughts involved in the poem are also personal.

Vaughan's escape from death by communion with God is not possible for Smith. Instead Smith, the modern metaphysical, attempts to secure his relief from death in Neo-Platonism or absurdist existentialism which holds that there is no fixed human nature and man is free to act according to his will. He deserts the ideal to choose the real. Hence in the poem the conventional religious symbols – "scab" and "wound," "angel" and "wing" implying crucifixion and resurrection – are ironically brought down to earth, to the grave, to nothing.

Watching the Old Man Die (1964)

It is a very practical poem of Smith who while watching an old man die thinks of his own death:

> Watching the old man die
> I savoured my own death
>
> . . . .
>
> When he struggled for breath
> With a kind of unhinged sigh
> I held my own in suspense.

Can there be any verse as realistic and down-to-earth as this? It is also very different in tone from his other companion poems on death as it winds back to the fear and depression expressed in "Journey" contrasting it with the sobriety of "On Knowing Nothing." Smith ends the poem with the following lines:

> The body cannot lie.
> I savoured my own death
> And wept for myself not him.
> I was forced to admit the truth.
> It was not his death I found grim
> But knowing that I must die.

My Death (1958)

"My Death" is an important poem in Smith's canon. It makes a death-wish, a desire to die. This desire is based not on withdrawal but on a higher level of acceptance because Smith is now fully conscious of the syncretism between life and death— "Nothing" and "All" – through his knowledge of Neo-Platonism and existentialism. The diction of the poem, again, is simple, swift and soft.

Death is described as sensuous and growing from a seed to flower:

> . . . My death is a thing
> Physical, solid, sensuous, a seed
> Lodged like Original Sin
> In the essence of being, a need
> Also, a felt want within.

Smith claims that death is as real as life. He gives a theological meaning for death and says that it is "a felt want within." He continues to give an account of Death's growth:

> It lies dormant at first,
> Lazy, a little romantic
> In childhood, later a thirst
> For what is no longer exotic.
> It lives on its own phlegm,
> And grows stronger as I grow stronger
> As a flower grows with its stem.

The death-in-life and life-in-death view is continued by revitalizing death by verbs like "lives" and "grows" and adjectives like "romantic" and "exotic" in this stanza.

But in the last stanza there is change of diction and attitude:

> I am the food of its hunger.
> It enlivens my darkness,
> Progressively illuminating
> What I know for the first time, yes,
> Is what I've been always wanting.

In this stanza, the poet identifies death as torch-bearer of life. He asserts that death is much more vibrant than life. He suggests that death and life are recurrent like a plant which grows, flowers and falls, only to be followed by another which it has seeded.

Sandra Djwa, basing her argument on the rhyme-pattern and metaphysical applications in the poem, has suggested "waiting" instead of "wanting" as the appropriate word in the last line. She states:

> . . . for Smith to have given the expected 'waiting' would be to acknowledge the difference between old metaphysics and the new, between the ideal and the real. It might not be unfair to conclude that it is Vaughan who is 'wanting' and that it is modern man who is waiting.
>
> ("Of Metaphysics and Dry Bones", 26).

The Wisdom of Old Jelly Roll (1978)

In "The Wisdom of Old Jelly Roll" the "All" of "To Henry Vaughan" finds an extension. The poem is in the nature of an Elizabethan sonnet with three quatrains and a rhymed couplet. The rhyme scheme is *abab cdcd efef gg*. In this poem the meaning of death as "nothing" and "everything" is explored through a metaphysical conceit which equates death with the holes in a net:

> . . . Parson, poetaster, pimp,
> Each acts or acquiesces. They prettify,
> Dress up, deodorize, embellish, primp,
> And make a show of Nothing. Ah, but met-aphysics
> Laughs; she touches, tastes, and smells
> - Hence knows – the diamond holes that make a net.

Jelly Roll's metaphysics triumphs over the parson, the poetaster and the pimp because they are bare and blank like nothing; but he would not "make a show of Nothing." The holes in a net are "nothing"; they are dependent upon the cord, a "thing," for their existence; the cord, in turn, is delineated by "nothing," and is intrinsically part of the one web. So are life and death. The lines that follow are a bundle of paradoxes:

> Silence resettled testifies to bells.
> 'Nothing' depends on 'Thing', which is or was:
> So death makes life or makes life's worth, a worth
> Beyond all highfalutin' woes or shows

To publish and confess, 'Cry at the birth,
Rejoice at the death.'

Thing and nothing, sound and silence, the net and its holes have meaning only in relation to each other. This wisdom of Old Jelly Roll, the blithesome black jazz musician, "On whiskey, ragtime, chicken, and the scriptures fed" is the most humanistic affirmation of death.

Metamorphosis (1957)

After experiencing fear and acceptance of death, Smith now upscales his poetry to a discussion of regeneration and rebirth. This is the subject of many of his later poems but nowhere with such intensity as in "Metamorphosis." It is a fourteen-line poem written in the sonnet tradition in a single sentence but it is not a sonnet. The human body battered and bruised by nature desires for death:

This flesh repudiates the bone
With such dissolving force,
In such a tumult to be gone,
Such longing for divorce,
As leaves the livid mind no choice

The "livid mind" is a wonderful phrase alluding to an enraged mind. Dissolution leads to amelioration and a new flower is born:

But to conclude at last
That all this energy and poise
Were but designed to cast
A richer flower from the earth
Surrounding its decay.

The newborn flower is a recycled object resulting from reductive metamorphosis because it is born from the decay of the old. Recognition has ended in regeneration. But, in this case, the regeneration is only provisional. Its transient nature is now emphasized:

And like a child whose fretful mirth
Can find no constant play,
Bring one more transient form to birth
And fling the old away.

Evidently it is the shrouding, the ever-raging death, that has attracted Smith's deepest poetic attention. It is natural that the psychophobic fear he describes in "Journey" and "Watching the Old Man Die" lead him to hallucinatory hostilities in "Prothalamium." He makes an incisive, anatomic description of death in "On Knowing Nothing" and "My Death." An awareness of inevitability of death makes him seek eternity in "The Two Sides of a Drum" and immortality through art in "The Archer." Finally, he shapes an acceptance in "To Henry Vaughan" which he elaborates in "The Wisdom of Old Jelly Roll." This acceptance is not based on religion, but on a mature belief in the rigidity of the natural order of things. The knowledge cycle ends with rebirth and regeneration in "Metamorphosis."

If Smith could be so coherent in his presentation of death it is because of his mastery of the seventeenth century metaphysical concepts. Smith placed profound faith in the metaphysical tradition. His characteristic poetic expressions are often drawn from the content of specific metaphysical poems. His central paradox "Glad to be Nothing, to be All," for example, draws verbally from Donne's "A Valediction of Weeping":

. . . On a round ball
A Workman that hath copies by, can lay
An Europe, Afrique, and an Asia,
And quickly make that, which was nothing. All.

In our analysis of various stages of Smith's poetry, we have identified four important segments. His earliest poems were absolutely romantic and rapturous, characteristic of a budding young poet. During the next phase of his career, he led a movement to develop an independent literary tradition for Canada through his readings of Eliot, Pound and the metaphysical poets when he practised classical modernism in his poems. He even revised his earlier poems to make them thoroughly classical. Consequently a characteristic duality of structure, combining romantic and classical elements, marked his poems of this period.

The third segment of his career is the period from 1935 to the end of the war, which was a period of interlude for him. He was at "two removes" from his characteristic philosophic and metaphysical poems. He wrote in a sort of ecstasy life affirming poems during this period of his career. During the last phase of his poetic career, Smith was preoccupied with the theme of death, where he approached death with acceptance and recognition.

7
Conclusion

Smith's poetry has a pattern. Knowledge of this pattern is essential to appreciate his poetry. This pattern is described here. Though Smith was a Canadian by nationality he was born of British parents. The romantic glow characteristic of Europe was inherent in him. But when he was a young man his youthful fervour for change and the agony of uncertainty in life coupled with his reading of Eliot and Pound made him a passionate prophet of modernism. The subsequent tension because of the coexistence of romantic and modern sensibility is the subject matter of Smith's earlier poetry.

During the thirties, when the period of personal uncertainty was all over and Smith was comfortably settled in life, his attention turned from self to society. This change in Smith is also historically significant because it is in correlation with the shift from depression caused negativism of the 1920s to the positivism of the 1940s. Still later, around the middle of the century, Smith shifted from social satires to life-affirming light lyrics. In his very mature age, the sobering influence set in, and he wrote metaphysical poems of great intensity on death and regeneration. His poetry needs to be reviewed in the background of this pattern.

Smith's poetry is a metaphorical journey from dissonance to assonance, from isolation to unification, from non-life to life. His imagist poems, for example, make a symbolic journey from agony to ecstasy. The disharmonious creaking note of "The Two Birds" undergoes a process of change and ends in an anthem of accord in "The Convolvulus." Similarly, in his earliest poems— "The Sorcerer," "The Journey" and "The Testament" – Smith finds solace for his sufferings in Christianity; but in his later poem "The Wisdom of Old Jelly Roll" he gets relief for his sorrow on Neo-Platonic and existential beliefs. Likewise, Smith's hallucinatory fear of death in his earlier poems "Journey" and "Prothalamium" mellows down to acceptance and regeneration in his later poem "Metamorphosis."

Smith's critical stance is in coincidence with this pattern. In the course of his energetic and enthusiastic defence of modernism in his early critical-pieces, "Wanted-Canadian Criticism" and "Rejected Preface to *New Provinces,*" Smith makes an aggressive criticism of the Confederation poets. Smith wanted to replace their poems with that of radical poets like Ross and Livesay in *New Provinces*. Again, when Sutherland, Layton and Dudek opposed his "native" and "cosmopolitan" distinction, he had to make concessions and work out a compromise. Smith had to recognize the special kind of cosmopolitanism these poets represented. When these concessions and adjustments were carried out in his own poetry, "inconsistency of the deep self" (George Woodcock: "A.J.M. Smith", 268) became the core concern of his poetry.

Smith is praised as a writer of serious, lapidary verse. He is accepted as an imagist, a lyricist, a social satirist, a fine translator and a metaphysical poet. But his extraordinary versatility is not generally recognized. Still worse, his versatility is set against him to charge him of shape-shifting. For example, Milton Wilson calls him the "Proteus-like Smith" (16). W.E. Collin describes Smith's poetry as "difficult, lonely music" (239). Gordon Harvey is the most volatile critic of Smith. Harvey declares: "A perpetual capacity for detachment and shape-shifting isn't individuality, nor does such a capacity fosters it" (25). Harvey claims that Smith's poems "lack depth of feeling and are derivative and dilettantish; their supposed difficulty is vagueness" (2). He further charges that Smith has been uncritically "canonized by acclamation and entirely on his own terms" (1).

One such canonization is that of Michael Darling who admits of inconsistencies in Smith's poetry but shies it away with this remark: "the paradox of the self that cannot choose is at the heart of Smith's best work . . . it is at the root of the classical-romantic debate" ("A.J.M. Smith", 268). Similarly, A. M. Klein defends Smith saying that "Smith has taken for his themes the grand verities and not the miniscule ephemera" (257). Though Smith's defenders like Darling and Klein have been sincerely attempting to free him of charges of inconsistency and shape-shifting, the charges are not wholly unfounded.

There are at least two occasions where Smith was inconsistent intentionally and shifting his position. The first occasion is related to the revision of his poems. The second is in relation to his genre shifting. The trend in his revisions is always toward the removal of romantic diction and the substitution of impersonal images and imaginative language. When "Proud Parable" first appeared in *McGill Fortnightly Review* in 1926 critics made a biographical reading of the poem. To appease the critics and make it impersonal Smith revised and published the poem in *Canadian Mercury* in 1928. Again he revised and published it in *Hound and Horn* in1932 with the addition of the important tenth line "O who is that bitter king? It is not I." In spite of the revision, W. E. Collin found the poem autobiographical. He wrote: "this poem is a perfect example of Smith's determination to turn his back on the world and lead an austere, aloof existence" (249). More recently, MacLaren wrote: "The old proud king is . . . an ideal to which the poet aspires" (62). MacLaren's opinion, suggestive as it is, merely confirms Collin's opinion. The poem "Testament" was first published in 1927. A revised version appeared in 1930, when the much-annotated line "I am not I, but a generation" was added to the text which is again typical of Smith's tendency towards "ironic self-mockery." In fact Smith's depersonalization revisions through modernist tools have neither appeased the critics nor gratified him.

The second occasion relates to genre-shifting. In an article entitled "Directions for Canadian Poets" published in 1936 Leo Kennedy accused Smith for "his failure to concern himself with socially conscious verse or social reality" (22). Immediately as if to set the scales right Smith published a series of social satires during the next decade. "Noctambule" appeared in 1936, "Far West" in 1939 and "Ode: The Eumenides" in 1942. But whether these poems are earnest expressions of Smith's social convictions is questionable. Pacey rightly points out that "the poems of social criticism of Smith are not sincere expressions of Smith's own convictions" (*Ten Canadian Poets,* 202). As a satirist, Smith was not one of those who believed that poets were the unacknowledged legislators of the world. His satires are mainly directed to manners. Amelioration was not his intent. Correction was not his purpose. Michael Darling writes: "His refusal to take a stand on the issues of the day marks him off from Scott, Kennedy and Dorothy Livesay" (quoted in Woodcock's *Canadian Writers and Their Works,* 12). W.J. Keith states that because Smith was "attracted to art through its premise of permanence, he was less directly concerned with social and political affairs" (*Canadian Literature in English,* 62).

Smith is a master of a wide range of styles: he uses pastiche, satire, burlesque, and bawdy. Yet his ribaldry gives way to simple lyricism and sensuality; he is on occasion meditative, and often colloquial. He is always authoritative, and always in quest of formal beauty, so that Woodcock speaks of him as being "among the most memorable lyric poets writing in the whole English-speaking world" ("A.J.M. Smith": *Canadian Writers and their Works,* 277). Northrop Frye discerns the same lyrical qualities in Smith, but feels the poems show a certain lack of energy. Smith's poems possess an aristocratic coolness and a shrinking from common vulgarities; they also show a singular joy in life and an uneasy fear of death. The life-game of love is subsumed in his bawdy. The world's irrationalities and aggressiveness are mocked, as in his poem "News of the Phoenix," or in his sarcastic verses on the atom bomb.

From the beginning of his poetic-career Smith has been trying to tell about human feelings and emotions but he never wanted to do that as a romantic. He writes:

> The 'I' of the poem, the protagonist of its tragedy or the clown of its pantomime is not me. As Rimbaud said, *Je est un autre.* I is another.
>
> ("A Self-Review": *Towards a View,* 213)

Smith adds a qualifying paragraph about the other side also. "The matter of poetic 'impersonality' is a little tricky in practice; the intelligence may choose what is to be expressed 'but what a lot escapes it – or cajoles it, or fools it!'" (214)

As a critic of his own poetry, Smith has always discouraged the identification of poet and persona. True to his feelings, critics of Smith have been writing "The speaker says" or "The persona of the poem says," never have they written "Smith says" or "The poet says." But, it is difficult not to submit to the temptation of identifying the poet and his persona. Leon Edel states that any poet's creativity is in part "a struggle between the presiding ego . . . and what manages to escape" ("The 'I' in A.J.M. Smith", 87).

In contrast to Smith's dictum *Je est un autre* is the following poem entitled "Prologue to a Poetry Reading: Address to the Audience" in which his idea of objectivity undergoes a see-saw reality. He begins the poem counselling impersonality:

I would like you to think of each poem
no matter how small
as a work of fiction
a drama
a myth
I am not I
not the I of the poem

certainly not –
at least not directly
the swaggering hero
or sensitive timid observer
who staggers or struts
through the action
and whose whispers or screams
you have come to hear.

Now, with a capitalized undercutting "BUT OF COURSE" Smith emphasizes the impossibility of removing personal feelings from a work of art:

BUT OF COURSE

under several layers of art
or artifice

and several layers
of subconscious compulsion
lurks
no one but I
the mole whose underground workings
these grassy or weedy hillocks
betray.

Smith is aware of both possibilities. A romantic at heart, he responded to the particular circumstances of his own career with a characteristic irony. It is this awareness which stresses the intellectual at the expense of the sensual that characterizes his poetry of the 1930s and 1940s. Some famous lines in the poems of this period can be construed as surrealist expressions of his unpleasant position – longing for one thing and yielding for another. In "Testament,"

I'm for the desert and the desolation.

. . .   .

Seeking a more difficult beauty
Unheartened by even the most faint mirage.

In "Proud Parable,"

And I will sing to the barren rock
Your difficult, lonely music, heart.

In "The Two Birds,"

I heard what that solitary cried
In a voice as twisted as mine.

And in "Cavalcade,"

He knew a good song, he knew a brave song.
But they stopped his mouth with the mud in Flanders.

such expressions of self-mockery are not found in his later poems. Smith allows the senses and emotion an equal share with intelligence in these poems. The lyrical evocation in "Wild Raspberry,"

> The eye feasts on them
> and feels refreshed

and in the paean of life in "The Convolvulus,"

> of the yellow sun
> and a million green shoots
> - in the communion of summer
> and the morning's glory

are noteworthy. In the poem, "To Frank Scott Esq. On the Occasion of His Seventieth Birthday," Smith lists the essentials of a good poet:

> To be a poet, Frank, you've shown
> is a harder thing. It is to be a stone,
> an eye, a heart, a lung, a microphone,
>
> a voice, but not a voice alone,
> a hand, a hand to grasp a hand, a leg to stand
> on, nerves to feel, and in supreme command
> the shaping mind that shapes the poem.

The list includes "an eye" to see, "a heart" to sympathize and "nerves to feel" – reserving a place for the "senses" in the poetic process. The self of Smith is a complex and split self, split between heart and mind, emotion and intellect which is obvious in his poetry.

Smith's eclecticism is much more than cultural cosmopolitanism. His eclecticism upholds the detachment of the artist and the notion that literature, even when it drew its material from experience, formed an autonomous world. Works of literature derived from other works of literature was a positive factor in his critical view and it extends into his creative practice also. This process of poetry reacting to poetry in self-conscious ways led to the creation of a kind of modernism, a metapoetics that anticipated postmodernism.

Since Smith wrote very short poems, the process of his progression from romanticism to classicism with its inevitable conflict becomes evident only when these poems are studied as a continuum. His early poems, written during 1922-25, "Quiet Haven," "Country Walk," "At a Fireside," "Vagabond" and "Vain Comfort" are romantic to the core. His later poems such as "The Crows" (1934), "With Sweetest Heresy" (1944) and "The Birches" (1967) are examples of the residual continuity of his romantic mood. But in the poems Smith published during 1925-40, the influence of T.S. Eliot, Pound and the metaphysical poets is observable. The conflict of "popular poetry he rejected" [romanticism) and "difficult poetry he valued" (classicism) is seen clearly in these poems. "The Two Sides of a Drum" (1926), "My Lost Youth" (1927), "Testament" (1927), "A Hyacinth for Edith" (1927), "Like an Old Proud King in a Parable" (1928), "The Creek" (1928), "Swift Current" (1930) and "News of the Phoenix" (1933) are some of the poems of this period. Even in the poems written after 1940, like "Metamorphosis" (1957), "My Death" (1958), "Watching the Old Man Die" (1964) and "The Wisdom of Old Jelly Roll" (1978) this conflict is evident but less markedly.

In style, Smith's poetry is a kaleidoscope of syllabic orgy ranging from tight, compactness of structure in "Shadows There Are" to the loquacious senility of "Brigadier," from sharp metaphysical imagery in "The Two Sides of a Drum" to the cool conversational manner in "News of the Phoenix." The sonnet form is his favourite. His "The Archer," "Angels Exist, and Sonnets Are Not Dead," "Bird and Flower," "The Cry," "The Plot against Proteus," "Poor Innocent," "The Mermaid" and "To the Christian Doctors" are all sonnets; the last two have variations in the sestet from conventional traditions. His metaphysical poem, "Metamorphosis," is a poem in fourteen-lines but with varied versification.

Smith is praised for his ironic diction indulging in hyperboles and paradoxes. But he is also said to lack clarity, which is because of concentration of a succession of images in a poem as in "Far West," leading the reader to oblivion; intertextual references to too many poets in a single poem, as in "Prothalamium"; a tendency to use the abstract for the concrete as in "The Archer," where an "arrow" is symbolized by thought: "The hissing arrow like a burning thought."

Smith's aims in poetry are sparseness, clarity, balance, the austerity of a classicism enriched by the discoveries of the symbolists and the imagists. As Louis Dudek states, Smith's "familiar poems form the big vertebrae and new poems constitute the smaller joints and tissue" ("A Load of New Books": *Selected Essays and Criticism* 168). He championed precise diction: "words / As crisp and as white / As our snow" ("To Hold in a Poem"). His poems are carefully worked out to the last moment involving an unending search for words that are crisp and sharp and small for a poem as "rare as his Phoenix and as terse as his knives" (Peter Hughes: "The Singers of Vinland", 64).

Smith's role in diverting Canadian poetry in the direction of modernism had nationalist consequences. It helped to get going the whole long movement of Canadian literature that had only come to maturity more than fifty-years after he fired the fuse that had led to what Frye called then, the "verbal explosion" ("Conclusion": *Literary History of Canada,* 318). If there is a period which it may be appropriate to describe as Canadian renaissance, it is eventually the time when Smith led his countrymen on a march to find their own language and their own voices.

Publication Details of Smith's Poems

Poems have been arranged in alphabetical order for easy reference. For those poems with change of title after their first publication, the latest, revised title has been alphabetized. Translations and adaptations have not been serialized.

Adolescence of Leda, The: *The Tamarack Review,* Autumn 1963.

Angels Exist, and Sonnets Are Not Dead: *The Canadian Forum,* April-May 1970.

Archer, The: *The Canadian Forum,* Jan. 1937.

Arp's Randy Rant in the Comfy Confession Box: *New Verse,* Dec. 1935.

Arts for Arts '25's Sake: *Old McGilll,* 1925. Signed 'Tomfool.'

Ascensions: *McGill Fortnightly Review,* 9 Jan. 1926. Signed 'Vincent Starr.'

Ascetic Who Found Another Way, The: *McGill Daily Literary Supplement,* 4 Feb. 1925. Signed 'A.J.M.S.'

Astra Redux: *Clv/n,* 1954.

At a Fireside: *McGill Daily.* "The Dilettante," 5 Dec. 1923. Signed 'T. F.'

Athletic Levy, The: *McGill Fortnightly Review,* 22 March 1926.

At Mycenae: *Michigan's Voices,* Winter 1961-62.

Ballade un Peu Banale: Appeared as "Pastorale" in *McGill Fortnightly Review,* 22 March 1926.

Beauty Dead: *McGill Daily,* "The Dilettante," 13 Dec. 1922. Signed 'S'.

Beside One Dead: *McGill Fortnightly Review,* 27 April 1927.

Birches at Drummond Point: *Quarry,* Summer 1967.

Bird, The: *McGill Fortnightly Review,* 22 March 1926.

Bird and Flower: Appeared as "A spiritual pigeon catapults thee," *The Canadian Forum,* Dec. 1944.

Bridegroom, The: *The Canadian Forum,* Jan. 1939.

Business as Usual: 1946: Appeared as "Business as Usual" in *Reading,* Feb. 1946.

Calvary: *The Rotarian,* April 1935.
Cavalcade: *The Canadian Forum,* Aug. 1928.
Chiroscuro: *McGill Fortnightly Review,* 20 Feb. 1926.
Chorus: *New Verse,* Aug.-Sep. 1936.
Circle, The: *Canadian Mercury,* April-May 1929.
College Spirit: *McGill Fortnightly Review,* 15 Dec. 1926.
Common Man, The: *The Canadian Forum,* Dec. 1945.
Conditional Mood: *McGill Daily,* 10 Jan. 1923. Published anonymously. Ascribed to Smith.
Convolvulus, The: *Pan,* No. 2, 1958.
Country Walk: *McGill Daily.* "The Dilettante," 7 March 1923. Signed 'S'.
Creek, The: *The Dial,* Nov. 1928.
Crows, The: *Poetry* (Chicago), July 1934.
Cry, The: *Poetry* (Chicago), April 1941.
Cry of a Wandering Gull, The: *McGill Fortnightly Review,* 5 Dec. 1925. Signed 'Vincent Starr.'
Danube 1922, The: *McGill Daily.* "The Dilettante," 7 Feb. 1923. Published anonymously. Ascribed to Smith.
Death and the Lady: *Canadian Poetry,* Nov. 1963.
Devil Take Her-and Them, The: *The Tamarack Review,* Winter 1963.
Dream of Narcissus, A: Appeared as "Narcissus" in *Contemporary Verse,* Fall 1951.
Eden's Isle: *Queen's Quarterly,* Winter 1956-57.
Epitaph: *McGill Fortnightly Review,* 9 Jan. 1926.
Epithalamium: *MonGrel Daily.* "The Dilly-Dally," 25 March 1924. Signed 'Damfull.'
Equestrian: *Delta* (Montreal) May 1963.
Etude in a Minor Key: *McGill Daily,* 15 Dec. 1926.
Face, The: *New Verse,* Aug.-Sept. 1936.
Faithful Heart, The: *The Right Review,* April 1939.
Far West: *Twentieth Century Verse,* Feb. 1939.
Felicity: *McGill Fortnightly Review,* 19 Dec. 1925.
Field of Long Grass: *McGill Fortnightly Review,* 27 April 1927.
Flame and Fountain: *McGill Fortnightly Review,* 15 Dec. 1926.
For Ever and Ever, Amen: *McGill Fortnightly Review,* 1 Dec. 1926.
For Healing: Appeared as "A Poem" in *McGill Fortnightly Review,* 22 March 1926.
Fountain, The: *The Adelphi,* Jan. 1934.
Good Friday: *Canadian Mercury,* March 1929.
Grecian Elegy: In *Poetry Yearbook 1925.* Montreal: Canadian Authors Association, 1925.

Hallowe'en: *McGill Daily.* "The Dilettante," 31 Oct. 1923. Signed 'Tomfool.' **Hellenica:** *McGill Daily Literary Supplement,* 19 Nov. 1924.

Here Lies an Honest Man: *McGill Fortnightly Review,* 23 Jan. 1926. Signed 'Vincent Starr.'

Humouresque: *McGill Daily.* "The Dilettante," 21 March. 1923. Signed 'S'.

Hyacinth for Edith, A: Appeared as "Homage to E.S." in *McGill Fortnightly Review,* 2 Feb. 1927.

Hymn of Hale, A: *McGill Daily.* "The Dilettante," 12 Dec. 1923. Signed 'Tomfool.'

Iliad for His Summer Sweetheart, An: *The Tamarack Review,* Autumn 1963.

In Memoriam: E.J.F.: *The Tamarack Review,* Summer 1964.

Interior: *McGill Daily Literary Supplement,* 21 Jan. 1925. Signed 'Vincent Starr.'

In the Churchyard at South Durham, Quebec: Appeared as "Two Epitaphs" in *McGill Fortnightly Review,* 27 April 1927.

In the City: *McGill Daily.* "The Dilettante," 21 March 1923. Signed 'S'.

In the Wilderness: *The Canadian Forum,* April 1930.

Irony: *McGill Daily Literary Supplement,* 4 Feb. 1925. Signed 'Vincent Starr.'

Jazz: *McGill Daily Literary Supplement,* 21 Jan. 1925. Signed 'Max.'

Journey: *McGill Daily.* 17 March 1926. Signed 'Michael Gard.'

Kindness to Animals: *McGill Daily.* "The Dilettante," 23 Jan. 1924. Signed 'Tomfool.'

Leda: *McGill Fortnightly Review,* 3 Nov. 1926.

Light o' Love : *McGill Daily Literary Supplement,* 4 March 1925. Signed 'Vincent Starr.'

Like an Old Proud King in a Parable: Appeared as "Proud Parable" in *Canadian Mercury, Dec. 1928.*

Lines Written on the Occasion of President Nixon's Address to the Nation May 8, 1972: *Poetry* (Chicago). Sept. 1972.

Little Death to Laugh About, A: *The Centennial Review,* Fall 1971.

Little Night Piece, A: *The Tamarack Review,* Autumn 1966.

Lonely Land, The: Appeared as "The Lonely Land: Group of Seven" in *McGill Fortnightly Review,* 9 Jan. 1926.

McGill Daily: *McGill Fortnightly Review,* 22 March 1926.

Mermaid, The: Appeared as "Legend" in *McGill Fortnightly Review,* 6 March 1926.

Metamorphosis: Appeared as "This Flesh Repudiates the Bone" in *The Tamarack Review,* Winter 1957.

Moment and the Lamp, The: *McGill Fortnightly Review,* 17 Nov. 1926.

My Death: *Queen's Quarterly,* Summer 1958.

My Lost Youth: Appeared as "Twilight" in *McGill Fortnightly Review,* 18 Feb 1927.

Narrow Squeak, A: *The Nation,* 1 June 1957.

News of the Phoenix: *New Verse,* Dec. 1933.

Nightfall: In *Poetry Yearbook, 1925,* Montreal: Canadian Authors Association, 1925.

Noctambule: *New Verse,* No. 22 (Aug.-Sept. 1936).

Nocturne: *McGill Daily Literary Supplement,* 21 Jan. 1925. Signed 'Vincent Starr.'

No Knife Needed: *Canadian Poetry,* Nov. 1963.

North Winds in September, The: *McGill Daily,* The Dilettante, 7 Nov. 1923. Signed 'S.M.'

Ode on the Death of W.B. Yeats: *Vice Versa,* Jan.-Feb. 1941.

Ode: The Eumenides: *Canadian Poetry Magazine,* Aug. 1941.

Ode to Good Form: *The Canadian Forum,* April 1931.

Offices of the First and the Second Hour, The: *New Verse,* Dec. 1933.

On Knowing Nothing: *The Nation,* 24 March 1956.

On Our Haste to Get Nuclear War-Heads: *Delta,* May 1963.

On Reading an Anthology of Popular Poetry: Appeared as "On Reading an Anthology of Modern Canadian Poetry" in *The Canadian Forum,* Dec. 1940.

On Reading Certain Poems and Epistles of Irving Layton and Louis Dudek: *The Canadian Forum,* May 1957.

On Reading Layton's "Poetry as the Fine Art of Pugilism": *Northern Journey,* June 1976.

On the Appointment of Ralph Gustafson, Esq. as Poet in Residence at Bishop's University: *The Tamarack Review,* Autumn 1966.

Pagan: *The Canadian Forum,* Sept. 1924.

Panic: *McGill Fortnightly Review,* 2 Feb. 1927.

Pastoral, A: Appeared as "Variations on a Theme of Cavalcanti" in *The Nation,* 15 March 1958.

Plot against Proteus, The: Appeared as "This is a theme for muted coronets" in *Hound and Horn,* Jan.-March 1932.

Poem: "Let us invert the world, and laugh." In *The Poets of the Future: A College Anthology for 1924-25.*

Poem: "When I was arrested for drunkenness." *McGill Fortnightly Review,* 18 Feb. 1927.

Poet in Residence: *Mitre,* 1966-67.

Political Intelligence: Appeared as "Political Note" in *Contemporary Poetry and Prose* (London), Nov. 1936.

Poor Innocent: Appeared as "The Natural" in *New Frontier,* Sept. 1936.

Poplar Leaves: *McGill Daily Literary Supplement,* 15 Oct. 1924. Signed 'Max.'

Portrait: *McGill Daily,* 24 Feb. 1926. Signed 'Simeon Lamb.'

Portrait and a Prophecy, A: *The Canadian Forum,* Dec. 1940.

Professor Windbag: *McGill Fortnightly Review,* 22 March 1926.

Prologue to a Poetry Reading: Address to the Audience: *Michigan's Voices,* Winter 1961-62.

Prothalamium: *The Dial,* July 1928.

Proud Parable: McGill Fortnightly Review, 6 March 1926. Signed 'S.'

Quiet Haven: *McGill Daily.* "The Dilettante," 21 Feb. 1923. Signed 'S'.

Quietly to Be Quickly: *New Verse,* Dec. 1935.

Requiescent: *McGill Daily Literary Supplement,* 3 Dec. 1924. Signed 'Corrinna.'

Resurrection of Arp: *New Verse,* April 1934.

Save in Frenzy: *McGill Fortnightly Review,* 20 Feb. 1926. Signed 'Vincent Starr.'

Sea Cliff: *The Canadian Forum,* June 1930.

Sermon: *McGill Fortnightly Review,* 10 March 1927.

Shadows There Are: *The Nation,* 15 June 1927.

Shepherd's Lament, The: *McGill Fortnightly Review,* 27 April 1927.

Shrouding, The: Appeared as "Hast Thee" in *McGill Daily,* 10 March 1926.

Silver Birch: *McGill Fortnightly Review, 6 Feb.* 1926. Signed 'S'.

Smile, The: *The Canadian Forum,* Feb. 1925.

Soldier's Ghost, A: *Poetry* (Chicago), July 1934.

Son and Heir: 1930: Appeared as "Son-and-Heir" in *New Verse,* June 1935.

Song against Constancy, A: *McGill Daily.* "The Dilettante," 12 March 1924. Signed 'Tomfool.'

Song: Made in Lieu of Many Ornaments: *The Tamarack Review,* Winter 1959.

Song, A: "My heart is like a garden." *McGill Daily,* 19 Dec. 1924. Signed 'Corinna.'

Song "O love, that you and I": *The Measure,* April 1925.

Song "O when the airs of April": *McGill Daily Literary Supplement,* 11 March 1925. Signed 'Max.'

Sonnet: "Although to-day no gleaming cavalcade." *Canadian Bookman,* June 1921.

Sonnet to a Bow-Legged Girl: *McGill Daily Literary Supplement,* 19 Nov. 1924. Signed 'Jay Ess.'

Sorcerer, The: Appeared as "Not of the Dust." *McGill Fortnightly Review,* 21 Nov. 1925.

Souvenirs du Temps Perdu: *here and now,* May 1940.

Speaking about Death: Blues for Mentor Williams: *The Tamarack Review,* Winter 1959.

Summer Warning: *McGill Fortnightly Review,* 6 Feb. 1926. Signed 'Vincent Starr.'

Surrealism in the Service of Christ: *Poetry* (Chicago), April 1941.

Swan and the Dove, The: *Michigan's Voices,* Winter 1961-62.

Swift Current: *The Canadian Forum,* June 1930.

Sylvan Rhapsody: *McGill Daily.* "The Dilettante," 1 Nov. 1922.

Symbols: *MonGrel Daily.* "The Dilly-Dally," 16 March 1923. Signed 'A.S.S.'

Tailpiece: *McGill Fortnightly Review,* 3 Nov. 1926.

Taste of Space, The: *Saturday Night, Nov:* 1966.

Testament: *McGill Fortnightly Review,* 10 March 1927.

Theology at the Symphony: *McGill Fortnightly Review,* 3 Nov. 1926.

They Say: Appeared as "The Woman in the Samovar." *McGill Fortnightly Review,* 5 Dec. 1925.

Thomas Moore and Sweet Annie: *Pan,* No. 2, 1958.

Three Phases of Punch: Appeared as "Punchinello in a Purple Hat" in *McGill Fortnightly Review,* 23 Jan. 1926.

Tit for Tat: *The Canadian Forum,* March 1960.

To an Old Tune: *McGill Daily.* "The Dilettante," 6 Dec. 1922. Signed 'S.'

To a Young Poet: *Poetry* (Chicago), July 1934.

To Evening: *McGill Fortnightly Review,* 27 April 1927.

To Frank Scott, Esq. On the Occasion of His Seventieth Birthday 1969: *McGill News,* Nov. 1969.

To Henry Vaughan: *The Tamarack Review,* Winter 1959.

To His Coy Mistress: *McGill Daily,* 20 Dec. 1923. Signed 'Tomfool.'

To Hold in a Poem: Appeared as "Prayer," *McGill Daily Literary Supplement,* 11 March 1925.

To Irving Layton, On His Love Poem to Mrs. Jacqueline Kennedy, Then First Lady: Appeared as "To Irving Layton on His Passion for the First Lady" in *The Canadian Forum,* April 1961.

To Jay MacPherson on Her Book of Poems: *The Tamarack Review,* Winter 1959.

To the Christian Doctors: Appeared as "Preceptors of the Heart" in *The Canadian Forum,* Dec. 1936.

To the Haggard Moon: *Pan,* No. 2, 1958.

Tree: *here and now,* May 1948.

Two Birds, The: Appeared as "Something Apart" in *McGill Fortnightly Review,* 1 Dec. 1926.

Two Sides of a Drum, The: *The Dial,* Dec. 1926.

Vagabond: *McGill Daily Literary Supplement,* 21 Jan. 1925. Signed 'A.J.M.S.'

Vain Comfort: *McGill Daily Literary Supplement,* 28 Jan. 1925. Signed 'S'

Walking in a Field, Looking Down and Seeing a White Violet: *Canadian Literature,* Winter 1963.

Watching the Old Man Die: *The Canadian Forum,* Jan. 1964.

Wave, The: *McGill Daily Literary Supplement,* 8 Oct. 1924. Signed 'Max'.

Wedding Night: *Delta* (Montreal), May 1963.

What is That Music High in the Air? *The Tamarack Review,* Winter 1957.

What Strange Enchantment: *McGill Fortnightly Review,* 21 Nov. 1925.

What the Emanation of Casey Jones Said to the Medium: *The Nation,* Jan. 1957.

When Thought of Her: *McGill Daily,* "The Dilettante," 31 Jan. 1923. Signed 'S'.

Wild Raspberry: *Pan,* No. 2, 1958.

Wisdom of Old Jelly Roll, The: *ellipse,* 1978.

Wistful Going, The: *The Canadian Student,* Nov. 1925.

With Sweetest Heresy: *Maryland Quarterly,* No. 2, 1944.

Ye Epicure Wisheth for Himself a Merrie Yuletide: *McGill Daily,* 20 Dec. 1923. Signed 'Tomfool.'

Bibliography

Primary Sources

Poetry Collections

News of the Phoenix and Other Poems. New York: Coward-McCann, Toronto: Ryerson, 1943.

A Sort of Ecstasy: Poems New and Selected. Toronto: Ryerson, 1954.

Collected Poems. Toronto: Oxford University Press, 1962.

Poems: New and Collected. Toronto: Oxford University Press, 1967.

The Classical Shade: Selected Poems. Toronto: McClelland and Stewart, 1978.

Essay Collections

Towards a View of Canadian Letters: Selected Critical Essays 1928-1971. Vancouver: University of British Columbia Press, 1973.

On Poetry and Poets: Selected Essays of A.J.M. Smith. Toronto: McClelland and Stewart, 1978.

Editorial Work

The Book of Canadian Poetry: A Critical and Historical Anthology. Chicago: University of Chicago Press, 1943.

Seven Centuries of Verse: English and American: From the Early English Lyrics to the Present Day. New York: Scribners, 1947.

The Worldly Muse: An Anthology of Serious Light Verse. New York: Abelard Press, 1951.

The Oxford Book of Canadian Verse: In English and French. Toronto: Oxford University Press, 1960.

Masks of Fiction: Canadian Critics on Canadian Prose. Toronto: McClelland and Stewart, 1961.

Masks of Poetry: Canadian Critics on Canadian Verse. Toronto: McClelland and Stewart, 1962.

100 Poems. New York: Scribners, 1965.

The Book of Canadian Prose: Early Beginnings to Confederation. Toronto: Gage, 1965.

Modern Canadian Verse: In English and French. Toronto: Oxford University Press, 1967.

The Collected Poems of Anne Wilkinson and a Prose Memoir. Toronto: Macmillan, 1968.

The Colonial Century: English-Canadian Writing Since Confederation. Toronto: Gage, 1973.

The Canadian Experience: A Brief Survey of English Canadian Prose. Toronto: Gage, 1974.

Smith, A. J. M. and F. R. Scott. *The Blasted Pine: An Anthology of Satire, Invective and Disrespectful Verse chiefly by Canadian Writers.* Toronto: Macmillan, 1957.

___ . *New Provinces: Poems of Several Authors.* Toronto: Macmillan, 1936.

___. A. J. M. and M .L. Rosenthal. *Exploring Poetry.* New York: Macmillan, 1955.

Articles

"The Poetry of W.B. Yeats." *The McGill Daily* 21 Nov. 1923: 3.

"Hamlet in Modern Dress." *The McGill Fortnightly Review* 3 Nov. 1926: 2-4.

"Contemporary Poetry." *The McGill Fortnightly Review* 15 Dec. 1926: 31-32.

"Wanted-Canadian Criticism." *The Canadian Forum* April 1928: 600-01. Rpt. in *Towards a View of Canadian Letters: Selected Critical Essays 1928-1971.* Vancouver: University of British Columbia Press, 1973: 167-69.

"A Note on Metaphysical Poetry." *The Canadian Mercury* 1 (Feb. 1929): 61-62.

"Refining Fire: The Meaning and Use of Poetry." *Queen's Quarterly* 61 (Autumn 1954): 353-64. Rpt. in *On Poetry and Poets: Selected Essays of A. J. M. Smith.* Toronto: McClelland and Stewart, 1977: 59-69.

"Eclectic Detachment: Aspects of Identity in Canadian Poetry." *Canadian Literature* 9 (Summer 1961): 6-14. Rpt. in *Towards a View of Canadian Letters: Selected Critical Essays 1928-1971.* Vancouver: University of British Columbia Press, 1973: 23-30.

"A Self-Review." *Canadian Literature* 15 (Winter 1963): 20-26. Rpt. in *Towards a View of Canadian Letters: Selected Critical Essays 1928-1971.* Vancouver: University of British Columbia Press, 1973: 211-16.

"The Poetic Process: Of the Making of Poems." *The Centennial Review of Arts and Science* 8 (Fall 1964): 353-70. Rpt. in *Towards a View of*

Canadian Letters: Selected Critical Essays 1928-1971. Vancouver: University of British Columbia Press, 1973: 217-30.

"A Rejected Preface." *Canadian Literature* 24 (Spring 1965): 6-9. Rpt. in *Towards a View of Canadian Letters: Selected Critical Essays 1928-1971*. Vancouver: University of British Columbia Press, 1973: 170-73.

"The Confessions of a Compulsive Anthologist." *Journal of Canadian Studies* 2.2 (May 1976): 4-14. Rpt. in *On Poetry and Poets: Selected Essays of A.J.M. Smith*. Toronto: McClelland and Stewart, 1977: 106-22.

"F.R. Scott and Some of His Poems." *Canadian Literature* 31(1967): 35.

"Light verse." *Princeton Encyclopaedia of Poetry and Poetics*. 2 nd. ed. Editor: Alex Preminger. Princeton: Princeton University Press, 1974: 448.

Secondary Sources

Aldington, Richard. *Life for Life's Sake*. New York: The Viking Press, 1941.

Anderson, David. (Tr.). *Pound's Cavalcanti*. Princeton: Princeton University Press, 1983.

Atwood, Margaret. *Survival: A Thematic Guide to Canadian Literature*. Toronto: Anansi, 1972.

Bagchee, Shyamal. "Problematizing the Modernist Novel: *Such is My Beloved* and *Swamp Angel*." *Canadian Literature: Recent Essays*. Ed. Manorama Trikha. Delhi: Pencraft International, 1994: 175-92.

Bentley, D.M.R. "Not of Things Only, But of Thought: Notes on A.J.M. Smith's Imagistic Poems." *Canadian Poetry: Studies Documents, Reviews* 11 (Fall-Winter 1982): 26-48.

Bergson, Henri. *An Introduction to Metaphysics*. Trans. T. E. Hulme. Indianapolis: Library of Liberal Arts, 1955.

Birney, Erle. "A. J. M. S." *Canadian Literature* 15 (Winter 1963): 4-6.

Brinin, John Malcolm. "Views of the Favourite Mythologies." *Poetry* 65 (Dec. 1944): 157-60.

Brooker, Jewel Spears. *Mastery and Escape: T. S. Eliot and the Dialectic of Modernism*. Massachusetts: University of Massachusetts Press, 1996.

Brown, E.K. "The Development of Poetry in Canada, 1880-1940." *Poetry* 58 (April 1941): 34-47. Rpt. in *The McGill Movement A. J .M. Smith, F.R. Scott and Leo Kennedy*. Ed. Peter Stevens. Toronto: Ryerson, 1969: 1-3.

—— . "A.J.M. Smith and the Poetry of Pride." *Manitoba Arts Review* 3.5 Spring 1944): 30-32. Rpt. in *The McGill Movement: A. J. M. Smith, F. R. Scott _ and Leo Kennedy*. Ed. Peter Stevens. Toronto: Ryerson, 1969: 95-98.

—— . *On Canadian Poetry*. Ottawa: Tecumseh, 1977.

___ . *Responses and Evaluations: Essays on Canada.* Ed. David Staines. Toronto: McClelland and Stewart, 1977.

Burke, Anne and Ellen Quigley. "A. J.M. Smith: An Annotated Bibliography." *The Annotated Bibliography of Canada's Major Authors,* Vol. 4. Ontario: ECW Press: 267-370.

Collin, W.E. "Difficult, Lonely Music." *The White Savannahs.* Toronto: Macmillan, 1936: 235-63.

Compton, Anne. "'After the ebb-flow': A.J.M. Smith's Nature Poetry." *Studies in Canadian Literature* 14.1 (1989): 54-72.

___ . *A. J .M. Smith: Canadian Metaphysical.* Ontario: ECW Press, 1991.

Darling, Michael. "An Interview with A.J.M. Smith." *Essays on Canadian Writing* 9 (Winter 1977-78): 55-61.

___ . "On Poetry and Poets: The Letters of W.W.E. Ross to Smith." *Essays in*

___ *Canadian Writing* 16 (1979-80): 78-125.

___ . *A .J. M. Smith: An Annotated Bibliography.* Montreal: Vehicule, 1981.

___ . "A.J.M. Smith's Revisions to His Poems." *Canadian Poetry: Studies, Documents, Reviews* 11 (Fall-Winter 1982): 7-25.

___ . "A.J.M. Smith." *Canadian Writers and Their Works, Vol. IV.* Poetry Series. Ontario: ECW Press, 1990: 232-287.

Davidson, Michael. *Ghostlier Demarcations: Modern Poetry and the Material World.* Los Angeles: University of California Press, 1997.

Dentith, Simon. *Parody: The New Critical Idiom.* New York: Routledge, 2000.

Djwa, Sandra. "Canadian Poets and the Great Tradition." *Canadian Literature* 65 (Summer 1975): 42-52.

___ . "'A New Soil and a Sharp Sun': The Landscape of a Modern Canadian Poetry." *Modernist Studies: Literature and Culture 1920-1940* 2.2 (1977): 3-17.

___ . "A. J.M. Smith: Of Metaphysics and Dry Bones." *Studies in Canadian Literature* 3 (Winter 1978): 17-34.

Dudek, Louis. "Reply to Envious Arthur." *Delta* 2 (Jan. 1958): 24-25. Rpt. in *Laughing Stalks.* Toronto: Contact, 1958: 43-45.

___ . "The Transition in Canadian Poetry." *Selected Essays and Criticism.* Ottawa: Tecumseh, 1978: 122-35.

___ . "'Aesthetic Master of Canadian Poetry.'" Rev. of *Collected Poems* by A.J.M Smith. *The Montreal Star,* Dec. 1962: 13.

___ . "A Load of New Books: Smith, Webb, Miller / Souster, Purdy, Nowlan." *Delta* 20 (1963): 27-28. Rpt. in *Selected Essays and Criticism.* Ottawa: Tecumseh, 1978: 168-74.

Edel, Leon. "Literary Revolution: The 'Montreal Group.'" In *The McGill You Knew: An Anthology of Memories,* 1920-1960. Ed. Edgar

Andrew Collard. Don Mills. Ontario: Longman Canada, 1975: 112-22.

___ . "The Worldly Muse of A.J.M. Smith." *University of Toronto Quarterly* 47 (Spring 1978): 200-13.

___ . "The 'I' in A.J.M. Smith." *Canadian Poetry: Studies, Documents, Reviews* 11 (Fall-Winter 1982): 86-92.

___ . "A.J.M. Smith." *The Oxford Companion to Canadian Literature*. Ed. William Toye. Toronto: OUP, 1983: 763-65.

Eliot, T.S. *Selected Essays*. 3rd ed. London: Faber and Faber, 1952.

___ . *On Poetry and Poets*. London: Faber and Faber, 1956.

Enck, John J. *Wallace Stevens: Images and Judgments*. Carbondale, Illinois: Southern Illinois University Press, 1964.

Ferns, John. *A.J.M. Smith*. Twayne's World Authors Series, No. 535. Boston: Twayne, 1979.

Fennollosa, Ernest. *The Chinese Written Character as a Medium for Poetry*. Trans. Ezra Pound. Washington: Square Dollar Series, 1935.

Francis, Wynne. "A.J.M. Smith." *Dictionary of Literary Biography: Canadian Writers,* 1920-1959, Vol. 88. II Series. Detroit: Gale Research Inc., 1989: 300-305.

Frye, Northrop. "Canada and Its Poetry." Rev. of *The Book of Canadian Poetry. The Canadian Forum, Dec*. 1943: 207-10. Rpt. in his *The Bush Garden: Essays on the Canadian Imagination*. Toronto: House of Anansi, 1971: 129-43.

___ . "Conclusion." In *Literary History of Canada*. 2nd. ed. Toronto: University of Toronto Press, 1976.

Fuller, Roy. "A Poet of the Century." *Canadian Literature* 15 (Winter 1963): 7-10.

Harvey, Gordon. "A.J.M. Smith and the Classical Shadow." *The Compass* 8 (Winter 1980): 1-28.

Heenan, Michael. "An Interview with A. J. M. Smith." 22 Dec. 2010. <http//www.uwo.ca/english/canadianpoetry/cpjrn/vol11/heenan.htm>

Hughes, Peter. "The Singers of Vinland." *Alphabet* .6 (June 1963): 63-64.

Hulme, T.E. "Romanticism and Classicism." *Speculations: Essays on Humanism and the Philosophy of Art*. Ed. Herbert Read. London: Routledge, 1924: 127-39.

Hutcheon, Linda. *A Theory of Parody: The Teachings of Twentieth Century Art Forms*. New York: Methuen, 1985.

Jameson, Fredric. *Postmodernism or the Cultural Logic of Late Capitalism*. Durham: Duke University Press, 1991.

Kearns, Lionel. "If there's anything I Hate It's Poetry." *Canadian Literature* 36 (Spring 1968): 67-68.

Keith, W.J. *Canadian Literature in English.* Toronto: Longman, 1985.

Kennedy, Leo. "Prufrock of Montreal, Que." *The McGilliad* 2.4 (Feb-March 1931): 87-88.

___ . "Direction for Canadian Poets." *New Frontier* 1.3 (June 1936): 21-24. Rpt. in *The McGill Movement: A.J.M. Smith, F.R. Scott and Leo Kennedy.* Ed. Peter Stevens. Toronto: Ryerson, 1969: 11-19.

Klein, A.M. "The Poetry of A.J.M. Smith." Rev. of *News of the Phoenix and Other Poems. The Canadian Forum,* Feb. 1944: 257-58.

Knister, Raymond. "Canadian Poems of the Month." *The New Outlook* 18 May 1927: 6.

Kokotailo, Philip. "Native and Cosmopolitan: A.J.M. Smith's Tradition of English-Canadian Poetry." *American Review of Canadian Studies* 20.1 (Spring 1990): 31-40.

Lakshmanan, V. "Conflicting Sensibility in A.J.M. Smith." *Seva Bharathi Journal of English Studies* 1.1 (Jan. 2005): 109-12.

___ . "A.J.M. Smith's Modernism: The Poetcraft of Twentieth Century." *Critical Essays: Canadian Literature.* Bareilly: Prakash Book Depot, 2004.

___ . "From Modern to Post-modern: A.J.M. Smith's Poetic Journey." *Critical Responses to Canadian Literature.* New Delhi: Sarup & Sons, 2004: 21-31.

___ . "Thomas Gray and A.J.M. Smith: A Comparison." *Journal of Annamalai University: Humanities* 40 (2002): 98-104.

___ . "Sharpness Cutting Sharpness: Imagism of A.J.M. Smith." *Critical Essays in Canadian Literature.* New Delhi: Sarup & Sons, 2003: 20-32.

___ . "Is Religion an Abracadabra in Smith?" *Politics of Survival: Studies in Canadian Literature.* Madurai: Jane Publishers, 1999: 57-62.

___ . *A.J.M. Smith as a Transitional Poet: A Study of His Modernism and Divided Sensibility.* Ph. D. Thesis, Annamalai University, India, 1998.

Livesay, Dorothy. Rev. of *News of the Phoenix and Other Poems. First Statement* 2.6 (April 1944): 18-19.

MacLaren, I. S. "The Yeatsian Presence in A.J.M. Smith's 'Like an Old Proud King in a Parable.'" *Canadian Poetry* 4 (Spring-Summer 1979): 59-64.

Malinowski. "The Social Psychology of Myth." *The Modern Tradition: Backgrounds of Modern Literature.* New York: Oxford University Press, 1965.

Mandel, Eli. "Life Sentence: Contemporary Canadian Criticism." *Laurentian University Review,* 10 (Feb. 1978): 7-19.

___ . "Masks of Criticism: A.J.M. Smith as Anthologist." *Canadian Poetry: Studies, Documents, Reviews,* 4 (Spring-Summer 1979): 17-28.

Marx, Leo. *The Machine in the Garden: Technology and the Pastoral Ideal in America.* New York: Oxford University Press, 1964.

Moore, Kathleen C. "'It is the Heart That Sees': An Interview with F.R. Scott." *Athanor* 1.2 (Feb. 1980): 5-10.

Nageswara Rao, T. *Inviolable Air: Canadian Poetic Modernism in Perspective.* Delhi: B.R. Publishing Corporation, 1994.

Nash, Walter. *The Language of Humour.* London: Longman, 1985.

Olson, Charles. *Selected Writings.* New York: New Directions, 1966.

Pacey, Desmond. *Creative Writing in Canada: A Short History of English-Canadian Literature.* Toronto: Ryerson, 1952: 124-27.

___ . Rev. of *A Sort of Ecstasy. The Fiddlehead* 25 (May 1953): 13-14.

___ . "A.J.M. Smith." *Ten Canadian Poets: A Group of Biographical and Critical Essays.* Toronto: Ryerson, 1958: 194-222.

___ . *Essays: Canadian Literature in English.* Powre above Powres, Series No. 4. Ed. A. L. McLeod. Mysore, India: Centre for Commonwealth Literature and Research, 1979.

Poggioli, Renato. *The Oaten Flute: Essays on Pastoral Poetry and the Pastoral Ideal.* Cambridge, Mass.: Harvard University Press, 1975: 1-41.

Pound, Ezra. *Selected Prose, 1909–1965.* Ed. William Cookson. New York: New Directions Publishing, 1975.

___ . "A Retrospect." Reprinted in *Modernism: An Anthology of Sources and Documents.* Ed. Kolocotroni et al. New York: University of Chicago Press, 1998: 368-79.

Pratt, E.J. "Canadian Poets in the U.S.A." *Canadian Review of Music and Art* 3.3-4 (April-May 1944): 35.

[illegible]senthal M.L. "'Poor Innocent': The Poetry of A.J.M. Smith." *Modern Poetry Studies* 8 (Spring 1977): 1-13. Rpt. "Introduction." *The* [illegible]*lassic Shade: Selected Poems* by A.J.M. Smith. Toronto: [illegible]Clelland and Stewart. 1978: 9-19.

[illegible] "Arthur James Marshall Smith: A Memoir." Symposium Papers, [illegible]higan State University, East Lansing, Michigan, 8 May 1976.

[illegible]th. *Aspects of Modern Poetry.* Rpt. St. Clair Shores, Michigan: [illegible]arly, 1972.

[illegible]ond. "Poems of W. W. E. Ross." *Experiment* 9 (1956): 23.

[illegible](ed.). *The McGill Movement: A.J.M. Smith, F.R. Scott and* [illegible]*dy.* Critical Views on Canadian Writers, No.2. Toronto: [illegible]9.

[illegible] of A.J.M. Smith." *Canadian Poetry: Studies,* [illegible]*views* 11 (Fall-Winter 1982): 1-6.

[illegible]Literary Colonialism." *First Statement* 2.4 (Feb. 1944): [illegible] *Essays, Controversies and Poems.* Ed. Miriam [illegible]on. New Canadian Library, No .81. Toronto: McClelland [illegible]ewart, 1972: 31-32.

[illegible]troduction: The Old and the New. Mr. Smith and the Tradition." [illegible]*ther Canadians: An Anthology of the New Poetry in Canada* 1940-46. Montreal: First Statement, 1947: 5-12

___ . "The Past Decade in Canadian Poetry." *Northern Review* 4.2 (Dec.1950- Jan. 1951): 42-47. Rpt. in *Essays, Controversies and Poems*. Ed. Miriam Waddington. Toronto: McClelland and Stewart, 1972: 70-76.

Traherne, Thomas. *Poems, Centuries and Three Thanksgivings*. Ed. Anne Ridler. London: Oxford University Press, 1966.

Waggoner, Hyatt M. *Americans Poets: From the Puritans to the Present*. Baton Rouge: Louisiana State University Press, 1984.

Wilson, Milton. "Second and Third Thoughts about Smith." *Canadian Literature* 15 (Winter 1963): 11-17. Rpt. in *The McGill Movement: A.J.M. Smith, F.R. Scott and Leo Kennedy*. Ed. Peter Stevens. Toronto: Ryerson, 1969: 127-35.

Woodcock, George. "Turning New Leaves." Rev. of *Collected Poems. The Canadian Forum*, Feb. 1963: 257-58. Rpt. in *The McGill Movement: A.J.M. Smith, F.R. Scott and Leo Kennedy*. Ed. Peter Stevens. Toronto: Ryerson, 1969: 120-25.

___ . "Smith's Hundred." *Canadian Literature* 15 (Winter 1963): 3.

___ . "Introduction." *Canadian Writers and Their Works, Vol. 4.* Poetry Series. Toronto: ECW Press, 1990: 5-25.

___ . "A. J. M. Smith." *Canadian Writers and Their Works, Vol. 4.* Poetry Series. Toronto: ECW Press, 1990: 231-86.

Index of Poems